PRAISE
THE GRADU

CW01510387

Scintillating, each paragraph packed with real-life experiences that answer the questions every twenty-first-century graduate is asking. Dr Odon is a storytelling maverick with a timely message.

Dr Anita Benson, Mandela Washington Fellow and founder of 'Embrace Melanin Initiative', Nigeria

Real-life experiences exposed for all. I recommend that every student and graduate has a copy in an attempt to create a better path for their future.

Victor Moinina, PhD student, Pan-African University Institute of Governance, Humanities and Social Sciences, University of Yaoundé, Cameroon

The Graduate Code made me realise the volume of resources I have within and around me, and how to utilise them to become the woman of my dreams. Reading it is a privilege for all students, fresh graduates and professionals.

Akunna Oyedum, communication specialist, Novartis, Nigeria

I could not drop this book. It forced a compelling mind-shift in me. Every student and professional who engages with this tool is set for a marked change in life. Well done, Dr Odon!

Bolanle Enang, MD, Capacity Growth Consult, South Africa

An exciting eye-opener on how to harness the opportunities available for both the unemployed and employed student. It has transformed my mind.

Caroline Atuzarirwe, Lecturer, Makerere University Business School, Uganda

As a former vice chancellor, chairman of the Inter-University Council for East Africa, and currently chair of the African Scientific, Research and Innovation Council, this is an eye-opener and a must-read book for all scholars, professors, students, professionals and the general public to better understand the intrigues and opportunities of attaining and utilising a degree.

Professor Ratemo W. Michieka, Kenya

This book contains so many simple codes to instantly transform a professional life. The government should have it as an instrument to fight against unemployment, every young person should read it before getting their degree, and for professionals, it's a must-have.

Caludia Togbe, PhD student in Public Law, electoral expert for the African Union, ECOWAS political governance and electoral consultant, and founder of cosmetics brand Origine Terre, Cotonou, Republic of Benin

Reading *The Graduate Code* gave me a sense of conscious direction. It is a book every student and graduate needs. As a postgraduate student it will help you take giant strides, bringing you closer to your destination with effective resources. Professionally, it serves as an awakening to resources and opportunities around you.

Afolakemi Ogunnubi, postgraduate researcher, Leeds University Business School, United Kingdom

Great empowering book for everyone, to develop the right mindset and to create the strategy in self-developing to become a future leader and entrepreneur. Through self-awareness, critical thinking plus knowledge-based evidence the book provides the power you need for your own success and determination.

Latifa Anda, EMEA International Business Development and co-founder of Mentor Lelo, Norway

Finally, my degrees, interests and hobbies can now share a table after I was introduced to *The Graduate Code*.

Adepeju Prince, school tutor, Nigeria

A captivating book that demystifies success for undergraduates, graduates and young professionals! Dr Odon shares a wealth of resources and amazing life experiences that are sure to cause a paradigm shift towards success! A must-read!

Rose-Margaret Ekeng-Itua,
Professor of Engineering,
Ohlone College, California, USA

The Graduate Code is a diagnosis of lived experiences, expectations and conflict between perceptions and reality. It's the architecture of a graduate's life and path to success.

Herbert Tato Nyirenda,
academic researcher/lecturer,
Copperbelt University, Zambia

I appreciated *The Graduate Code* for its fascinating explanation of the baffling subject of entrepreneurship. This is a breath of fresh air for all young people and graduates, teaching them that trying new things can be scary but fulfilling.

Cisante-Charles Dzimwasha, business reporter at Zimpapers
and journalist at the *Zimbabwe Mail*, Zimbabwe

In my eyes, *The Graduate Code* has the unique ability to answer the most important and recurrent questions raised by millennials on job opportunities and what is helpful and needful in career pathways for generations to come.

Lionel L. G. Issombo, student, BA Politics and International
Relations, Lancaster University, Ghana

Timely, relevant, thought-provoking… Dr Odon's keen insight could not be more useful to the burgeoning youth population of Africa. Relatable, as he shares his own experience which is universal across our continent. A must-read if you want to be part of the new wave of the African Renaissance.

Natasha Omokhodion-Banda,
entrepreneur and Lusaka MD
of 99c Advertising, Zambia

Dr Odon's compelling account is experiential, thought-provoking and crisp. A pertinent compass for students at the cusp of their professions and professionals embedded in their careers. *The Graduate Code* is a mentorship companion I wish I had as a student and hope every student can have.

Lily Mburu, lawyer, scholar and
governance consultant, Kenya

I have seen Dr Odon at work many times and it is a joy to behold. Whether inspiring students about their careers or corralling a room full of vice chancellors and chief executives into challenging their preconceptions, his boundless energy, keen insights and deep love for Africa are infectious. This is exactly what he captures in *The Graduate Code*, a book for all.

Ibrahim El Mayet, Regional Business Development Manager,
Middle East and Africa, University of London, United Kingdom

A guidebook, a compendium, the ultimate code, a must-read. Well now, 'the constitution' that every graduate should read, reflect on and adopt, for a successful career. Dr Odon, Africa and indeed the world will be forever indebted!

Mohammed Ruwange, Oil and Gas Faculty Lead,
Strathmore University Law School, Kenya

What a fascinating read. *The Graduate Code* provides an abundance of practical and multilateral examples on how to strategically plan beyond a degree and study for a career ahead. A must-have book for all university students and professionals.

Krisztina Morris, founder of Plan b Public Relations and corporate social responsibility lecturer, University of the Sunshine Coast, Australia

Akanimo Odon has done a tremendous service with this work. *The Graduate Code* is an influential book, essential reading for young people interested in bridging the gap between what society throws at them and what they could be. It offers a timely message to twenty-first-century students and graduates faced with diverse challenges that threaten their academic and professional path.

Stephanie Linus, actress, director, producer and founder, Next Page Productions, Nigeria

A necessary read for both graduates and professionals who are ready to step out of their comfort zone and take control of their career path in an ever evolving job market. Aimed specifically at Africans but with lessons for all, this book actively explores several career options to enable individuals reach their full potentials.

Lizzie Anoliefo, Project Lead at the Department of Education, United Kingdom

The Graduate Code is a must-read for everyone who is interested in not re-inventing the wheel of knowledge and experiences but just oiling it for a great career. The author has dealt so well with the subject matter to the extent that the book can be used as a career textbook.

Stan Deh, Banker and Sustainability Professional, Stanbic Bank, part of the Standard Bank Group, Ghana

THE GRADUATE CØDE

In every professional is a student wanting to learn
and in every student is a professional waiting to earn

DR AKANIMØ ØDØN

First published in 2019 by the Independent Publishing Network
Copyright © Dr Akanimo Odon, 2019

The moral right of Dr Akanimo Odon to be identified as the author of this work has been asserted by him in accordance with the Copyright, Designs and Patents Act 1988

ISBN: 978-1-78972-055-6

Typeset by Tetragon, London
Printed and bound in Great Britain by TJ International Ltd, Padstow, Cornwall

This book is dedicated to my lovely wife, Ifeyinwa,
for bearing with me as I travel all over the world,
and to my amazing kids, Kaela and Kanaan.
I love you guys!

CONTENTS

. . . .

PART I: CRACKING THE GRADUATE CODE

. . . .

PART II: APPLYING THE GRADUATE CODE

· ·

PART III: ENHANCING THE GRADUATE CODE

ABOUT THE AUTHOR

Dr Akanimo Odon holds a first-class honours degree in zoology from the University of Benin in Nigeria, a master's degree in environmental rehabilitation from Aberystwyth University in the UK, a PhD in environmental management from Lancaster University in the UK and business and enterprise certifications and fellowships from Cambridge University in the UK and Stanford University in the USA.

While his specialism is cross-border education and research in the environmental and extractive industries, Dr Odon has a wealth of experience in different sectors. He navigates, develops and manages relationships between academia, government and industries in Africa, focusing on economic viability, the impact of research, and graduate employability. As a member of the National Student Forum, he acted as an adviser to the British government on developing international education policies, later working for the British Council as an education consultant. He also spent two years as a business development consultant for the Grow Creative Scheme under the European Regional Development Fund (ERDF), and worked as Africa Strategy Adviser for Aberystwyth University and the University of East Anglia, both in the UK.

Dr Odon is currently African Regional Adviser in the UK for the University of London, Lancaster University and the University of Strathclyde. He recently founded FlexyLearn (www.flexylearn.com), a one-stop online shop for distance-learning provision for Africa.In the last ten years, Dr Akanimo Odon has organised and hosted over 100 international workshops and conferences, liaised and collaborated with government, industries and academia in over 30 African countries, developed more than 100 strategic educational, research and commercial partnerships between UK and African organisations, facilitated and supported the setting up of over 20 African-focused SMEs, designed and implemented over 40 strategic capacity-building and knowledge-transfer schemes and programmes, delivered innovative career impact and management workshops to more than 5,000 young professionals and delivered graduate-enhancing talks to over 30,000 students and graduates, on the back of which he has launched the Graduate Enhancing Programme for Africa (GEPA).

The Graduate Code is a book resulting from his experiences engaging with students, young graduates and professionals in Africa and internationally.

WEBSITES: www.akanimo-odon.com; www.flexylearn.com
LINKEDIN: https://www.linkedin.com/in/drakanimoodon
TWITTER: @AkanOdon
FACEBOOK: Akanimo Odon
INSTAGRAM: @Akanimoodon
HASHTAGS: #thegraduatecode #akancareertours

FOREWORD

It is a great honour and a delight to have been asked by Dr Akanimo Odon, an erudite scholar and one of a kind, to contribute to the Foreword of *The Graduate Code*, a lucid, helpful and well-researched guide to help graduates make the most of their future careers. *The Graduate Code* is a testament of overwhelming significance and a 'one-stop shop' for personal growth.

As a close associate of the author, whom I have known for upwards of 20 years, I can authoritatively speak on the quality and relevance of this book and attest to its insightful, intriguing and instructive content. The uniqueness of *The Graduate Code* as a metaphor is found in its credibility and phenomenal compass for graduate transition.

One of the greatest difficulties confronting all graduates is the problem of adjustment to life 'outside the box'. *The Graduate Code* is a brilliant combination of intuitive thoughts and common realities, and links divergent perspectives to help graduates work their way towards a successful career.

This book is a must-read, and is certainly not one to be left on the shelf. It is a compendium of national significance and global importance. It contains all it takes to provoke the educated as well as the uneducated to aspire to greater heights in life. It is against this background that I highly recommend *The Graduate Code* for life after higher education.

Professor Lawrence Ikechukwu Ezemonye, PhD, FNES, FSESN
Professor of Ecotoxicology and Environmental Forensics
Vice Chancellor
Visiting Professor, Lancaster University, UK
National President, Nigerian Environmental Society (NES)

It is indeed a great honour to be asked by the author, Dr Akanimo Odon, to contribute to the Foreword of *The Graduate Code*. I have known Dr Odon for 14 years, initially as my first African PhD student, later as a collaborator on many African projects and now, most importantly, as a great friend. As a young researcher, he was always involved in several activities, many of which had nothing to do with his PhD. He has not changed; his energy remains boundless, we have had many interesting adventures together, and, at least in part, I have been privileged to watch him work with young Africans. It is very impressive to see him in action!As he says in this book, over the last 15 years he has led over a hundred Africa-focused international workshops and conferences, worked with government, industries and academia in more than half of the countries on the African continent, developed numerous partnerships between UK and African organisations, etc. But I think the most important impact has been his work with and the training he has delivered to thousands of young Africans. Most recently, Dr Odon has been a key contributor to several multi-million-pound international projects which bring researchers from the UK and all over sub-Saharan Africa to work together on important and impactful trans-disciplinary research.

I would like to think that I have a good appreciation of Dr Odon's energy, enthusiasm and vision, coupled with his understanding and expertise in graduate training and development, so it comes as no surprise to me that Dr Odon has put 'pen to paper' to produce this insightful and highly readable guide for graduates to develop beyond their time at university. *The Graduate Code* is a book which has emerged from his experiences in engaging with young Africans in Africa and overseas. Although the focus comes from Dr Odon's observations and experiences in Africa and is primarily for African students, the narrative is applicable to all students and young professionals to enhance their careers.

This is a highly readable and practical handbook to help students and young professionals think about and plan their career using the resources already available to them. The subtitle of the book really does hit the nail on the head.

Professor Kirk T. Semple

Professor of Environmental Microbiology and Director of International Engagement, Lancaster University, UK

Visiting Lecturer at the University of Benin, Nigeria

Fellow of the Cooperative Research Centre for Contamination Assessment and Remediation of the Environment (CRC CARE), Australia

PREFACE

The ultimate intention of studying at university is to either get a job or start a company and live a valuable (and valued) life after graduation. But if there is little focus on how to do that while still at university, don't you think we have a problem? Note that I use the word 'university' loosely here to refer to institutions of further education which could be polytechnics, colleges of education, technical institutions or universities in the traditional sense. With *The Graduate Code*, I hope to speak directly to students of these institutions, new graduates and others who have completed their studies within the last ten years: young working professionals, including those running their own businesses, and even those in further education.

I have been asked a lot lately about my own career journey, so before beginning, I thought I would share my experiences with you. I am blessed and I know it well, and so gratitude to God comes easy. I scored 204 in the Nigerian Joint Admissions and Matriculation Board (JAMB) examinations, the official entrance examinations to get into any first degree course, but my score was far too low. As a result, I was unable to take up a place studying Medicine, as I had originally planned. However, I was accepted onto a Zoology course. I managed to get a scholarship for my master's degree in England and afterwards, with minimal funding, I registered for a PhD. I worked as a cleaner, pot washer and carer in an elderly care home while studying. Then I won five international awards including best international student in the UK, wrote and published two books, co-founded an NGO that convened the largest conference of Nigerian students in the UK, founded a small consulting firm, undertook programmes from Cambridge, Stanford and Lancaster Universities and obtained a doctorate, all by my 27th birthday.

Now I consult for global universities, I advise numerous governments, international firms and agencies and my consultancy liaises with more than 30 African countries.

You will notice that I have not mentioned the failures and heartaches along the way, my mistakes and missteps, the ups and downs of my journey, the secrets and insights I have learned or the choices I made and the opportunities I have missed. The truth is, if I had known then what I know now, my career path would have been very different, and a lot smoother. I have written *The Graduate Code* so you can avoid the same pitfalls while at the same time taking advantage of the booming opportunities all around you.

Education is generally believed to be instrumental in reducing poverty, and graduation should be the foundation for building a career. When – as currently seems to be the case – an increase in the number of graduates stymies economic growth and hinders graduate career progression, it becomes a major problem. In Africa, as in many countries, we seem to be losing the essence and importance of what it means to be a graduate.

In an attempt to break this negative cycle, this book is a fresh attempt at developing a 'graduate code', a set of ideas and suggestions to help you make the most of your time at university and the years after graduation.

The book is made up of three main parts, each containing several chapters. Each chapter is made up of three subsections: a summary of the tenets (i.e. the main messages) for that chapter, an in-depth code narrative and some practical activities. These activities are designed to get you to engage with the code and take responsibility for your own career progression. For it to work, you will need to keep an open mind and respond to each activity honestly. I hope that *The Graduate Code* will help you to think a bit more carefully about your graduate career.

HOW TO USE THE GRADUATE CODE

1   Read the tenets of each chapter carefully and try to get a sense of the message of the chapter. Do not worry so much if the message of the tenets is not immediately obvious, as it will be when you read the code narrative. You might need to refer back to the tenets once in a while to understand their connection with the narrative.

2   Read the code narrative of each chapter to appreciate the full message and insights that bring the tenets to life. Note that these narratives have been developed from personal experiences and the experiences of friends, colleagues and acquaintances. The idea is to use the code narrative to build a picture and consider how it relates to your past or present situation.

3   Each chapter's code narrative will prepare you to respond to the practical exercises that follow. Try to respond to these exercises as much as possible – even if the essence might not be clear to you, it will become clearer as you progress. There are two blank lined pages at the end of every chapter, which you can use to respond to the practical exercises. I realise these two pages might not be enough to fully respond to all the practical exercises, so feel free to include extra sheets within the pages and keep them safe. This is important because even though the codes in every chapter are separate, they are all closely interlinked, and you will be asked in some cases to refer back to previous answers when responding to new ones.

4   Finally, keep an open mind, be ready to engage and trust the process, and I wish you a good read as you delve into the Graduate Code!

ACKNOWLEDGEMENTS

Firstly, I would like to thank God for His grace. It has been an absolute pleasure to write this book, but it would not have been possible without the help and support of a few very important people. So may I use this opportunity to acknowledge my amazing parents and siblings, for all their love and encouragement. And Mum, I feel the power of your prayers every day. Thanks to my two mentors – Professor Lawrence Ezemonye and Professor Kirk Semple, who have been bombarded with my career challenges for upwards of 15 years. I don't know how you guys put up with me, but at least you still agreed to write the book's foreword. Also thanks to my pastor, Ian, and his lovely wife Geraldine, and to my entire family at Kings Community Church, Lancaster, for their guidance and love. This book is filled with praise, case studies and experiences, and so thanks to my friends, colleagues and everyone who responded to my questionnaires and opened up their lives which informed this book. Special thanks to Sarah Terry and Alex Billington, my professional editors, for agreeing to take this on. I hope you both had fun. Finally thanks to my family for believing in me against all odds – and extra special thanks to my daughter Kaela for coming up with the concept for the book cover.

PART I

Cracking the Graduate Code

· ·

*This part introduces the underlying basis and
significance of the Graduate Code, and explores the
graduate career crises we face and the responsibilities
on our shoulders to change the status quo.*

CHAPTER 1

Introducing myself

. . . .

THE TENETS

1.1 Do not focus too much on the course, but rely a great deal on the force of the course. It is always a plus.

1.2 Success and the love of it, is – or at least is supposed to be – a universal ambition of all. Seek it with all you've got.

1.3 In a highly competitive professional world and an unemployment-ridden society, graduate differentiation is literally everything. Make it a thing.

1.4 Why would you want to struggle through your studies and fumble after graduation? Get it together and avoid career stumbles!

1.5 No one likes the idea of spending extra to retrain a student who has already been trained. What is the point?

. . . .

I am often asked what I do for a living, and I used to pause for a moment to consider how best to articulate it, eventually giving a fumbled response. I would instantly be aware that I hadn't expressed myself clearly when the enquirer immediately asked 'So what does that mean?' or 'But what does that involve?'

These people must have wondered how I could be unable to express clearly and succinctly what my professional role was, especially when I had been doing it for over seven years. This was not because it was unclear to me (or to the person asking), but because my job was totally and 'interestingly' unique. Over the years I have got better at understanding what I do and am supposed to be doing, and as a result, I find it easier to explain. So when you ask me now what my role involves, I simply say, 'I am an international business consultant and I advise and support foreign organisations in developing and managing their Africa strategies. I also support African organisations to develop and manage their internationalisation strategies.'

Basically, I am the middleman, the navigator, the connector (recently, friends have referred to me as 'Mr Africa' and 'Mr Fix-it', for obvious reasons). A funny and less obvious name that I have been called a lot recently is 'Ajala'. Before you ask what that means, it is a dialect word in Nigeria, where I hail from, used to address a wanderer par excellence. I travel an awful lot around the great African continent, imbibing its beauty and grace along with its challenges and failures. Africa is a continent made up of 54 countries, and my humble 'Ajala-self' can say that I have visited, liaised with and developed strategic partnerships in 36 of those countries over the space of seven years. I have some more catching up to do before I have completely circumnavigated the continent!

I connect Africa to the rest of the world, and vice versa. When an African-focused or Africa-based project or programme is being conceptualised, my job is to analyse the intricacies and potential challenges involved and how these can be addressed and mitigated for. I have become an expert at articulating strategic partnerships between African and foreign institutions, and helping maintain these intriguing (and sometimes intimidating) institutional relationships is now second nature to me.

If you have a question at this point, it is probably something along the lines of 'Did your degree course directly relate to what you now do for work?' or 'Were the skills you need for your job something you learnt at university?' The answer to both questions is no; there are no courses I know of titled 'Africa Business Strategies' or 'Africa/ UK Partnership Management'. However, everything I do has been chosen with care and sometimes organically developed through my graduate exposures, experiences and experimentations.

Since I mentioned the word 'graduate', you are now probably wondering what I studied in school. Okay! Here we go…

I studied for my first degree, a BSc (Bachelor of Science) in zoology, at the University of Benin, Nigeria, graduating with first-class honours. After this, I went on to study for a master's degree (MSc) in environmental rehabilitation at Aberystwyth University in the UK and then completed a PhD in environmental management at Lancaster University, also in the UK.

So how are all these qualifications connected with my current role?

Well, for starters, they are a testament to the well-known fact that it is not what you studied in school that counts, but what you made of it. As I like to put it, it is not 'your course' but 'your force' which drives the direction your life takes. (Pardon the *Star Wars* analogy; I've just got a thing about rhymes.)

In most African countries, there used to be many more public universities than private ones. This trend has started to change as more private universities have been built in order to meet increasing demand in higher education. In Nigeria, with a population of more than 180 million people, there are about 167 universities, of which 100 are public (federal and state) while 67 are private. In Kenya, there are 22 public universities, 14 chartered private universities, and 13 universities with a letter of interim authority. In terms of student population, the public universities make the private ones pale into insignificance. The common denominator with public universities is that they are heavily subsidised by the government, giving students from average and low-income homes the opportunity to go to university – which they frequently do. In my first-year class at the University of Benin, I was one of those students: my father was a civil servant and my mother was a petty trader. With four of my other siblings already at university or wanting to go to university, my parents' hands were already full of responsibilities.

My point here is this:

A good and successful university experience opens up the possibility of a more successful life after your studies. To get that dream job, to start that groundbreaking enterprise, to buy your parents their first car or to say a big thank you for the effort they put into enabling you to go to university, is the expectation. In Africa, it is a general, cultural and even spiritual expectation that children should take care of their parents. It is what parents long for and boast to their friends about. 'My child is at university,' they proclaim with their heads held high, waiting hopefully for the rewards when they are no longer strong enough to work. In a society such as in most African countries, with no national insurance or government welfare system in place, where older people depend on insignificant and often insufficient pension payments, this child-dependence factor is fundamental. And this applies to those in the civil service; don't get me started on discussing the precarious situation most other people find themselves in.

Interestingly, this is also the case for many students from high-income and rich families whose parents insist they study at a public university in their home country for their first degree to ensure 'proper cultural integration' and 'national enlightenment'. There is usually the added promise of studies overseas for their postgraduate education, which differentiates them from most other students. Or does it? You will have to wait till Chapter 20, 'Optimising opportunities for internationals', to find out more. Anyway, my point here is: is overseas study relevant and a source of pride if you are still completely dependent on your parents after completing your graduate studies? Should you be proud of being incapable of taking over the family business despite having completed your studies? In a sense, whether you are rich or poor, it is what you put into – and get back from – the course you study and your time at university that differentiates you from the bunch, not the course subject itself. And trust me, in a highly competitive business world and unemployment-ridden African society, graduate differentiation is literally everything.

I need to make it clear that I am an unrepentant advocate of taking care of parents and the have-nots in society. However, I don't believe that this should be the principal driver of a successful student or postgraduate life, irrespective of cultural pressure. I believe that success in life improves people's self-worth, sense of personal value and makes them feel fulfilled, and that this in turn benefits those not so fortunate. That is a more sustainable premise.

Here it would be unforgivable to forget the others who have had to pay their own way through university through thick and thin and endless disappointments. For these people, shouldn't the need to get it right be even stronger? Why would you want to struggle to complete your studies and continue to struggle after graduation? If you're not willing or able to put in the effort to make more of yourself, you might as well not go to university at all – four or five years of university education is a long time to be playing the fiddle. But what if you *can* get it right?

Irrespective of your societal or economic status as a student, one thing remains principally true, and that is that success and the love of it is – or at least is supposed to be – a universal ambition of all.

These days, you cannot afford to sail through your undergraduate life with an utterly nonchalant attitude. Understandably, most students want to do well after they graduate, but do they take the necessary steps to ensure that they do? And in African states and higher institutions, a laid-back attitude to university studies is an even bigger risk. The higher education system in Africa, unlike in many other places, is not (or rather, has not been) structured to enforce or integrate the steps needed to ensure a successful graduate career, thus adding to the complexity of the Graduate Code.

In the UK, for instance, universities measure part of their success by the percentage of alumni employed after graduation. This illustrates clearly how much of their own force students have put into their time at university. The mere fact that graduate employment is a measure of university standard, reputation and student impact, means that processes have been put in place at many universities to almost guarantee this. It becomes a great selling point in choosing a university. This is an ideal situation. And rightly so, considering the reasons for going to university in the first place.

I'm sorry to tell you this, but Africa – and indeed several developing economies – do not have the luxury of 'ideal situations'. African universities, on the whole, tend not to promise graduate employment (or graduate employability, at least). Traditionally, the act of going to university has been seen as making graduates employable. There is a real danger that many students apply to university simply because that is what is available to them within their resources – or because they are expected to go – and not because they are motivated to make the most of themselves and be successful after graduating.

The number of university graduates has more than tripled in Africa over the last decade, but so has the graduate unemployment rate. If graduates are well prepared to be employable, this shouldn't be the case. This situation is indeed worrying and scary!

The government of the day is expected to create jobs for their citizens. This is what they promise in political campaigns. In order to get re-elected, they talk about bringing unemployment levels down. Unemployment levels are so important that global organisations such as the World Bank and the International Monetary Fund (IMF) use them as an indication of whether a country or economy is successful.

Now I might be wrong here, but I can't remember where and when there has been focus on *employability*. A government or organisation can create lots of jobs, but if people don't have the right skills to take on those jobs, doesn't that defeat the purpose? Creating employment should be backed up by creating employability. One possible reason for this disparity is that some governments believe that it is their responsibility to create employment but someone else's responsibility to create employability. Presumably this is where universities and educational institutions should fit in. But how well do they do this job? You need to ask the employers if they think universities have fulfilled their roles and guess what? I have, and the answers have not been very positive. No wonder we have pre-employment programmes, graduate employment schemes, retraining initiatives, corporate induction activities and summer schools for young employees.

And that reminds me – I have also jumped on the bandwagon and developed the Graduate Enhancement Programme for Africa (GEPA), which focuses on getting graduates to think about careers way before they leave education. This book you are now holding forms one of the strands of that grand scheme. But I digress.

A quick question, if I may: Do you think employers want to spend extra to retrain a student who has already been trained? I doubt it. If graduate employment and employability is crucial but the powers that be are unwilling to help, is it unreasonable to expect someone else to take on that responsibility? Who do you think should take responsibility, especially in today's critically competitive environment? Guess who? YOU.

Believe it or not, this book is an attempt to decipher the ambiguity and current professional confusion facing the graduate and how that translates to their lives and career pursuits and progression.

It has been envisaged as a guide for young people, written from another young person's candid perspective, to ensure their employability after graduation.

That is me still thinking I am a youth. Humour me! This book has become an enormous weight on my shoulders that must be lifted for the survival of the graduate species. The DNA restructuring and evolution of a new generation of graduates has never been so important. The time to break ancient habits and to develop a new code is now. Walk with me, and let's make a start on Activity 1.

. . . .

ACTIVITY 1: GETTING TO KNOW YOU

I hope you feel you know me now you have finished Chapter 1. It would be good if you could return the favour and tell me about yourself. So let's begin!

1a. Write a professional-sounding description of yourself *as you are now*, in no more than 100 words. What impression would your description give potential employers?

1b. Now try writing a professional-sounding description of *your future self*, in no more than 100 words. How does this differ from your answer to 1a?

NOTES

NOTES

CHAPTER 2

Introducing the Graduate Code

. . . .

code (noun): a system used for brevity or secrecy of communication, in which arbitrarily chosen words, letters or symbols are assigned definite meanings.

Dictionary.com

. . . .

THE TENETS

2.1 In the huge elephant tussle of mismanaged educational systems, the students and graduates, like green grasses, are always the losers. Be aware.

2.2 If you dislike your programme, change it; if you can't change it, accommodate it; if you can't accommodate it, align with it, because all in all, there is goodness in every programme. There is always the availability of multiple career directions, but it is their accessibility that you need to work on.

. . . .

This definition of code implies a complex item or situation which requires ingenuity to decipher. But how is this relevant to you? Let me explain.

Irrelevant as it might initially sound, it is actually a good description of Africa's educational system, which is effectively a huge collection of stakeholders made up of proprietors and beneficiaries, assessors and regulators, all pulled together and apart in seemingly random directions. In this 'elephant tussle', the students and graduates, like the green grass on which the elephants stand, are the ones who lose out.

Frequent academic strike actions, constant disagreements between those in different circles, educational migration on one end and cultism on the other: all make this code more complex. Unfortunately, alas, many foreign educational institutions take advantage of this state of confusion by perpetually advertising 'better' educational (and sometimes 'asylum') opportunities in the national dailies. And who would choose to go overseas if the educational system at home was good (unless, of course, they wanted something extra such as global exposure or a different academic environment)?

There is no simple answer, no all-encompassing formula from worlds unknown, and I will not pretend that I have all the answers. After all, the code we face at the moment is quite complex. However, what I do know is that the current code can be dismantled just enough for a new set of codes to be developed. This time I refer to the governing principles behind the Graduate Code, which aims to guide you through university and to a successful graduate life.

As I have been delivering guest lectures to student bodies and interacting with graduate groups in different African countries, something has become very clear to me. Believe it or not, but it seems that one of the biggest challenges they face is ignorance, and sometimes just plain naivety.

You would be wrong if you thought this situation was unique to students and graduates living in Africa, though. After engaging over the years with undergraduate and postgraduate students and young professionals living, studying and working in the UK, I have seen that the situation is not so different. Ignorance still remains a fundamental challenge, and the truth is that people just don't know how to make the most of their time at university in order to make themselves employable after graduation.

But I am glad to say that the situation is not totally hopeless.

Recently, I was delivering a career talk titled 'The Graduate Code' (surprise, surprise!) to over 200 undergraduate students at the University of Benin, Nigeria, and I felt incredibly jealous. I stood there, jealous at how they didn't even know how blessed they were to be hearing what I was saying. I couldn't help wishing that someone had told me these things when I was in their position – fresh, young and protected from the chaos of professional life in that incredible career-building, life-changing and profession-shaping bubble known as university.

At one point, I started asking questions, and requested a show of hands so I could gauge the dynamics in the room. 'How many of you are currently studying a subject you dislike?' I asked. About half of the room put their hands up. Then I asked the next question: 'How many of you have decided to stick with the programme (course) that you now do, even if you dislike it?' And a third of the room put their hands up. Then I asked the final question: 'Who here knows what they want to do when they graduate?' and only four students put their hands up. I appreciate that these were only around 200 students out of the 40,000 at that particular university, but I have seen the same trend in several African countries when asking the same questions of different groups of people.

Let's put this in perspective.

On the one hand, around half the students I spoke to wished they were studying something else but were compelled by the system to continue with it. On the other hand, around a third of students had decided to focus and complete their studies despite not being satisfied with their course. But what got me the most is that even the majority of those who loved their courses still had no idea what they wanted to do after they graduated.

As I mentioned in Chapter 1, I studied zoology at university, but this was not my intent when I took my entrance examinations. I wanted to study medicine, and my parents were delighted at this idea. Being called 'Dr Akanimo Odon' sounded really cool to me (naively, the idea of saving lives was an afterthought!). I needed to score 250 in the official undergraduate entrance examination to be accepted to study medicine. As you might remember from the first chapter, I only scored 204. My dreams (or rather, what I assumed were my dreams at the time) were crushed. Instead of medicine, I was directed to register for a course I knew nothing about.

I know this is a situation many are familiar with, and I will cover this topic in a later chapter, but I wish to make the point here that it is not the course you study that is important but the force you bring to it. Going by the minuscule number of students who showed their hands when asked if they knew what they wanted to do after graduation, it re-emphasises my view that the real issue is understanding what you want to study after graduation well enough to prepare for it. And even if you don't know exactly what you want to study, might it not still be a good idea to plan for what might lie ahead?

Now, let me tell you some more about my case, in the hope of you noticing some parallels to your situation.

In my second year of studying zoology, I took a module called Environmental Management. I had a professor who was a dynamic and impressive lecturer (and at the time he drove the best car in the department, so this caught my attention). I asked around and was told that he was a consultant to the oil and gas company Shell and that he also did consultancy work for a few other oil and gas firms. Everyone knows that oil and gas firms are the highest-paying employers in any oil-producing economy, and I remember thinking, 'I also want to work for an oil and gas firm.' It was the first time in the two years of my course that I realised that studying zoology didn't mean I would need to work in a zoo after graduation. Instead, the module on environmental management, just a small part of my course, inspired me to change the direction my career was going in. And if I couldn't work in environmental management, I had a fallback plan to become a lecturer (provided, of course, that I graduated with first-class honours). So in some sense I already had two potential career directions even in my second year: environmental consultancy for oil and gas firms, or lecturing. No wonder I went on to do a master's degree in environmental rehabilitation and a doctorate in environmental management. Currently, I am an environmental consultant, an adjunct lecturer in environmental law at a top private university (and yes, I have also worked for several oil and gas firms). I guess you now see where this is going.

In my professional opinion, it is always better to understand and appreciate the availability of multiple potential career directions and to focus on developing one or two, with the potential to develop more later if they fit well with your objectives and capacity. There are always many possible careers you could go into, but you need to work on making these accessible to you.

Undergraduate students may love what they are studying, dislike it intensely or feel undecided about it, but they are never given information about the possible directions their career might take after graduation. As a result, many students end up unsure what will happen after they graduate. At this point I can categorically say that every course or programme leads to a multitude of different careers *if you are guided appropriately*. And if there is no one there to guide you, you need to act as your own guide.

With this in mind, let's try Activity 2 now. For young professionals who are already embarked on a career not linked to the course they studied, this activity will still be of value. I know many people who have changed the direction of their career completely and started in a new field. After all, you spent more than three years at university, and even if your professional life is not currently connected with your undergraduate course, it still can be.

When you have finished, take a look at your answers. Are they similar to and compatible with the answers you gave to the questions in Activity 1? If they are, congratulations! You have already started moving towards a career which is tied to your course of study, and my next step will be to show you how to arm yourself with the right resources to jump-start that amazing career using the Graduate Code. (You will probably also need to consider other potential career directions, and Chapter 4 of the Graduate Code focuses on this.) If what you have written in Activity 2 is totally different to that in Activity 1, it means that you already have multiple possible career directions in front of you, which is an incredible position to be in!

. . . .

ACTIVITY 2

2a. (Undergraduates/those still studying) Considering your current programme of study, write down three possible directions you see your career going in after you complete your studies.

2b. (Graduates and professionals only) Knowing what you now know, write down three possible directions your career could have taken after graduation.

NOTES

CHAPTER 3

Taking the bull by the horns

· ·

THE TENETS

3.1 The best time to start to plan what you might want to do after graduating is before you actually graduate. If you have already graduated, the best time to plan is now.

3.2 For career success, the things we need we don't have; the things we have we don't need; and the things we need and actually have, we don't use. Get the things you need, let go of the things you don't and use the things you've got.

3.3 You need to learn about the national, regional (continental) and global career trends and demands of your course (programme).

3.4 Knowing your career space helps you to develop your relevance to fit in place.

· ·

For you to appreciate the significance of the Graduate Code, I need to paint you a really graphic but true picture of Africa's higher education system. In addition to this, I need you to realise how crucial it is to have a panoramic view of national, continental and even global career sectors, opportunities and agendas while thinking about the direction your career might take. If there is no demand for workers in a particular sector, change your focus – there is no point wasting your efforts.

The best time to start to plan what you might want to do after graduating is *before you graduate*, and I will explain why.

In many African countries, there is a huge gap between academia and industry. In other words, there is a disconnect between what is studied at many universities and what employers want. It is important to give you a sense of how much of an issue this disconnect is so that you can appreciate the need to take the bull by the horns.

To give you an example, Nigeria is the most populous country in Africa, with over 180 million people. As such, it also has the largest number of higher education institutions, the most graduates annually, the most unemployed graduates and… You get the picture. In Nigeria, the oil and gas industry has been the economic mainstay for over 40 years, and you would expect postgraduates in this sector to have completed their studies in Nigeria. But no, most concluded their postgraduate education overseas, in places such as Scotland. Security has been a big issue in Nigeria for a long time – Boko Haram in the north and the Niger Delta insurgence in the south – but yet less than 5% of Nigerian universities offer any truly international undergraduate or postgraduate programme in security management or strategy.

'Nollywood', Nigeria's film industry, is the third-highest producer of movies in the world, after Hollywood (USA) and Bollywood (India). However, only a handful of universities offer a top-notch international programme in film-making. The telecommunications sector is huge in Nigeria – as it is in several African countries – yet virtually no universities offer an undergraduate or postgraduate programme in telecommunications, which makes no sense.

Most universities in Nigeria offer zoology as a course. Since I was at university the course seems to have been renamed in many institutions, but the fact remains that there are very few zoos in the country. In addition, there is no clear career guidance for zoology students, and so a tiny percentage of those who study the subject end up doing anything zoological. Little wonder that the first job I did after completing my studies in zoology was working in a bank, and I probably would have continued in my banking career if other factors had not intervened. The same is the case for students who studied chemistry, botany, microbiology, librarianship…the list goes on.

With the current drive for food security and environmental sustainability, the majority of Nigerian universities offer agriculture as a course of study, but a tiny minority of agriculture graduates actually end up working in the sector, meaning that Nigeria continues to import over USD 2 billion worth of food annually. Every Nigerian university now has an environmental programme at undergraduate level, but again only a tiny minority of its graduates actually do anything environmental. If I have got this right, we don't have the things we need; we have things we don't need; and we don't use the things we both have *and* need.

Although I wrote the above paragraphs about the Nigerian higher education system, in many respects they describe the higher education system across Africa. As a graduate, your game plan should be to counteract this summary and thrive by making yourself distinct from other graduates. How might you do this? By making sure you get the resources and information you need, let go of what you don't need and use the resources you already have. If you can do this, you will be just fine.

According to the World Economic Forum, the world's ten youngest populations are all in Africa. Uganda, for instance, has one of the youngest populations in the world, with a median age of about 16.

With a population of 42 million, 77% of the Ugandan population are less than 30 years old and about 42% are less than 15 years old. That is remarkable. The sad part here is that youth unemployment stands at over 83%, and of those employed young people, over 90% are in the informal vocational skills sector. Of the remaining young people who have jobs, only 3% work for employers and 7% are self-employed. Uganda's oil and gas industry has developed rapidly in the last couple of years, and there is currently a shortfall of around 25,000 people with the relevant vocational skills needed to work in this sector. As a result, the country with the largest future labour potential could easily end up becoming the country with the largest labour crisis if nothing changes. Innovative people will see opportunities in adverse situations such as these, and this is the premise of the Graduate Code.

It is crucial to emphasise that every course of study has many potential career directions, and that it is vital to understand the 'career landscape'. Let me focus here on two of the most important employment sectors in Africa at the moment, which are likely to remain major employers for some time: agriculture and IT.

Did you know, for example, that the agriculture sector and agro-value chains in Africa, if properly harnessed, can reduce poverty two to four times faster than any other sector, with a projected value of one trillion US dollars and the ability to create up to 17 million jobs in Africa by 2030? However, over 70% of agriculture graduates work in unrelated sectors. If agriculture is the next big topic in Africa – and going by the current policy direction of the African Union, Africa Development Bank and many African countries, it certainly looks that way – then we have a problem on our hands.

Information technology is also a major employer, and the ability to use computers and software applications is an economic game changer. To illustrate this, a quick look at my mobile phone shows that I have a total of 93 mobile apps installed. Of these apps, a closer look shows that only four of these are by African developers. (You can probably guess which these are – the mobile banking apps.) Take a look at your mobile phone for a minute. Does it reflect this trend? I know that most African universities offer computer science as a programme, but how many offer software engineering or IT enterprise management? By talking to people in this sector, I have realised that the few young IT gurus we have either taught themselves core software programming or app development through liaisons with established IT firms, or studied at foreign institutions. (My older brother is a case in point. He taught himself everything he knows about software engineering and landed a high-level job in Australia.)

My point here is that there is no excuse for naivety or ignorance. You need to learn about national, continental and global trends and the skills needed in relation to your programme of studies while you are within the protected walls of the university – once you have graduated, life (particularly working life) can be chaotic. Knowing your space helps you to develop your relevance so you can find your place in the career world.

With all this in mind, let's look at Activity 3. Here, I want you to start researching information relating to your course and its associated career trends. It should begin to connect you with the world of graduate employment.

. . . .

ACTIVITY 3

3a. Based on data, figures and/or trends in *your country*, use credible resources and reliable internet sites to outline five important and relevant points related to the course/programme you are currently studying (or the course/programme you studied).

3b. Based on data, figures and/or trends *on your continent and/or globally,* use credible resources and reliable internet sites to outline five important and relevant points related to your course/programme (or the course/programme you studied).

....

....

....

....

....

....

....

....

....

....

....

....

....

....

....

....

....

....

....

....

....

....

....

CHAPTER 4

Choosing your career route(s)

. . . .

THE TENETS

4.1   There are three graduate career routes: employment, enterprise or education. Choose today which route(s) you're best suited for and for when.

4.2   Why would you want to spend so many years doing something you didn't like, only to quit and start something you did like, if you could spend a little more time planning for something you do like so that you don't have to quit at all?

4.3   The lack of a clear direction is always a good foundation for an easy resolution when confronted with career obstruction. The trouble is people often resolve to do something within their comfort zone but somewhat mediocre in comparison to their potential.

. . . .

It would be particularly unfair to assume that everyone has a knack for being entrepreneurial. In the same vein, it would be unfair to assume that everyone wants to work for an employer. Personally, I have always known that I wanted to set up something of my own and that I never wanted to work for an employer. I didn't particularly know how that was going to happen, though. Maybe if I had, things would have been a lot different. That doesn't mean that I didn't end up working for a few employers – and to be honest, even now I run my own consulting firm, I have regular clients who I consult and advise. Though they share clients, they could also be seen as my employers, but not in a 9 a.m. to 5 p.m. working hours sort of way.

Some people feel they are born to be employers, while others function better when working for someone else. Irrespective of your choice or disposition, preferring one to the other doesn't limit or reduce your capacity for graduate success; neither does it mean you have not fulfilled your graduate ambitions. From what I know now, though, I would say that it is important to be aware of (or at least to get a sense of) which you prefer, as this will influence the decisions you make about the career you wish to pursue.

A common interview question, and one you may already have been asked, is 'How do you see yourself and your career ten years from now?' This has always felt like an intrusive question to me: what business of theirs is it? It seems especially odd being asked this before graduating, especially when the answer you want to give is 'I don't even know what I want to do when I graduate one year from now, and you are expecting me to tell you my plans a decade away?' However, there is another way you can look at it. Consider this instead: if, while you were still studying, the same question was asked during a pre-interview for a job that was not yet advertised, what would your answer be?

You hear all the time about people who spend years working for an employer (or series of employers) before deciding to resign and set up their own companies. And you probably know people who finished school and decided to start their own businesses – because they couldn't find a job, rather than because they had any entrepreneurial motivation – and then, a few months down the line, started looking for employment again. I bet you've also heard of people graduating, working for an employer for a while, then leaving to run their own business for a while before eventually deciding to return to further education.

Those examples take me nicely to the three E-routes post-graduation: Employment, Enterprise and (further) Education. In other words, after graduating you can either work for someone, work for yourself or study some more. (There may well be people who ask, 'What if I don't want to choose any of those routes?' This response would allow for a fourth E-route I would like to call Entitlement. Yes, you do have a trust, a never-depleting fund, some huge reserve left for you by your parents and you don't need to worry about ever working or even studying. It is not a common situation in Africa – or indeed anywhere else – but let's permit it for the sake of completeness.)

I spoke about these E-routes at a forum and someone said, 'Hey, doc, you forgot another E-route.' I asked what it was, and she replied, 'Engagement.' I didn't see that coming! I guess some might argue that this option is only valid if getting married propels you towards a progression in your career, but for the sake of my sanity, let's stick with the three main E-routes.

With that said, it is important to note that no one route is superior to the others – and neither are any two routes mutually exclusive. In fact, they are inextricably linked. For me, I had to work for some-one for a while to learn how to work for myself, and I had to study further to better understand what I was going to specialise in, and why I wanted to specialise in the area I now work in.

You might wonder why considering and appreciating these routes appropriately is an important dimension of the Graduate Code. The question I wish to put to you in response is: 'If you were able to take your career in the direction you wanted right from the start, just by spending a little more time planning beforehand, would you instead choose not to plan and spend years working in a job you disliked?' It's all about perspectives, clarity and aligning your interests and goals.

During my undergraduate years, I was totally clueless.

After graduating with a first-class honours degree in zoology, I did my compulsory one-year graduate National Youth Service Corp (NYSC) programme at the now defunct Platinum Bank in Nigeria. Six months in, the idea of having a career in the banking sector had begun to appeal to me, and I was doing well in the marketing unit, recruiting new clients for the bank. I well remember those frequent visits to Shell in Warri, south Nigeria to pitch banking products to its senior staff members. The idea of working in banking became even more appealing when I realised that this was a blessing, especially when I was not particularly sure what I was going to do with my zoology degree. A part of me always retained a love for environmental management – but since I was unclear at this stage if I wanted to work for someone or undertake postgraduate studies in that exciting field, working in a bank was an easy option. I believe that I would have made a good career in the banking sector, but I don't think I would have found as much joy in it as I do in my present role. While I was working for Platinum Bank I lacked a clear direction, which is a good way to end up stuck in the wrong career. I want you to have the tools to step out of this comfort zone and embrace your potential.

Don't get me wrong – I know the challenges many people face, not to mention how hostile the environment can be, and I'm aware that sometimes people feel they have to make do with what is readily available. But however naive it might sound, I maintain that settling for less means you can't try for the best. It may sometimes be difficult to find the right environment to make your plans happen, but if you have no plan, you cannot take advantage of opportunities that are aligned with that plan. When you fail to plan, you plan to fail.

While I was serving at Platinum Bank, I visited my dad's office library, and I stumbled across an old Association of Commonwealth Universities catalogue. Remembering my love for environmental management and without any prompting, I drew up a list of UK universities. I literally followed it in alphabetical order, so I ended up applying to the University of Wales in Aberystwyth, the University of Aberdeen, Bangor University and a few others under the letters A and B in the alphabet. I was pretty naive, as you can see, and didn't bother looking at the whole range of universities available to me.

I remember not telling anyone (not even my parents!) that I had applied; and to be honest, I had no particular expectations. For starters, there was no way I would be able to afford overseas study! However, a few things *were* clear to me. Firstly, I had chosen to apply to these universities. Secondly, I had applied to study a master's degree in environmental management in all the UK universities I had applied to. Thirdly, I had begun to consider further studies as a possible postgraduate route (if by some divine arrangement I actually got a scholarship to study overseas). And fourthly, I still had a possible banking career ahead of me if all else failed. As naive as I was in many ways, I still had a sense of career direction and a plan, even if these were totally uncoordinated and lacking strategic insights.

I ended up following the further education route (by progressing on to a master's degree and a PhD) and then returned to a short stint in employment before finally setting up my own enterprise. However, all this was totally unplanned. Imagine how I might have been able to plan if, by some sci-fi magic or hindsight, I could have gone back to my second year at university knowing the things I know now! That question of 'How do you see yourself and your career ten years from now?' would be articulated with utmost relish and perfect clarity.

But then that's me daydreaming. It is unrealistic to expect to plan ahead in a crisp and clear fashion, and for every aspect of your future career to be mapped out, but some sense of a plan is always better than none. The real trouble is that many current students or young graduates have no plan whatsoever and simply drift with the wind. But why would you choose to drift with the wind when you have access to a sail? If you completely avoid thinking about your future career, you run into real problems.

Maybe you don't know yet how to go about considering your options. If this is you, try not to worry. Just having some sense of which of the post-graduation routes you wish to take – or being aware of how to gradually combine the different options open to you – and understanding the direction your career could take in the professional landscape (whether national, continental or global), puts you a notch above ignorant. And if you have even a vague sense of direction, this will enable you to take some clear steps in advance of graduation.

I know you will want to know the outcome of my application, so here it is… One fateful day in July 2003, I received an email. Paraphrasing, it read, 'Dear Akanimo, you have been awarded a full commonwealth scholarship to study for a MSc in Environmental Rehabilitation at the University of Wales, Aberystwyth,' and the rest is history. Interestingly, Platinum Bank offered me a full-time job the same week I got my scholarship letter. I think you know by now which option I chose!

Let's move on now to Activity 4, and think about your longer-term plans.

. . . .

ACTIVITY 4

4a. How do you see your career in the next ten years?

4b. If you were to map out or mini-plan your career around employment, enterprise or further education, what might it look like? More importantly, why would it look this way?

PART II

Applying the Graduate Code

....

This part comprehensively outlines the core tenets of the Graduate Code, and focuses on the main issues you need to understand to help you plan a great graduate career.

CHAPTER 5

Getting paid for your hobbies

· ·

hobby (noun): an activity that someone does for
pleasure when they are not working.

Cambridge English Dictionary

· ·

THE TENETS

5.1 There is a difference between what you love to do
and what you're paid to do. It's probably okay to do
what you're paid to do but wouldn't do unless you
were paid. However, while you're doing what you're
paid to do but wouldn't do unless you were paid, it's
crucial to invest time and limited resources developing what you love to do and would do even if you
were not paid.

5.2 When you get paid to do what you love and would do
even if you were not paid, this epitomises the 'dream
job'.

5.3 Universities provide the perfect environment to start
or develop a hobby you enjoy or an interest you love.
Run with this, because it's a possible career direction.

· ·

If I understand the above definition right, your hobby is tied to work inextricably – except that it is the release from work. (In other words, your work is the thing you will be paid to do which stresses you out so much that you need a hobby to relax.) It might be right to assume that the more you hate your job, the more stressed you are likely to get, and the more likely you are to become dependent on your hobby.

This then leads me to the next question: can a hobby stress you out? Think about that for a minute. I hope not, because that would totally defeat the purpose of a hobby, wouldn't it? You might then need another hobby to release you from the stress of your stressful 'hobby'. (Anyway, let's not let me mess with your mind.) My point is that a hobby is something you enjoy. If you don't, it won't serve its purpose. But imagine this scenario: what if you could be paid to do your hobby?

I am sure you will have been asked 'What hobbies do you have?' many times. (It is a particularly important question to ask during a date. I doubt you would go on a date and not want to find out a bit about the other person's hobbies!) But why is the question important in the context of your life and career post-graduation? Let me tell you.

There is often a difference between what you love to do and what you are paid to do. It won't do you any harm to do something you would only do if you were paid – but if this is the case, it is crucial to invest your limited time and resources developing what you love to do (and would happily do even if you were not paid). Trust me, the Graduate Code is all about helping you find your 'dream job', in other words the career where you are paid to do what you love.

It is important to note that I use the term 'hobby' loosely in this chapter to mean anything you enjoy doing that is not what you are studying – or studied in the last few years – but which has the potential to be a career direction. Can all hobbies be developed into a career direction, though? Perhaps, given the right support, focus and resources. (This question is particularly personal to me. I used to love long-distance running when I was in high school. I wasn't particularly great at it, but it was something different. Unfortunately, I had given it up by the time I went to university. However, even if I had continued with athletics in university, I am not sure I would ever have considered long-distance running as a career. Maybe if I had I would have run in the Olympics. Yeah, right!)

The point is that I spent Part I of this book writing about how you could progress your career on the back of your school and university studies but didn't consider outside interests. How about we spend some time analysing your other interests and how they could possibly lead you to your future career?

When I look at my daughter, I see a ten-year-old girl who is learning and developing several different interests or hobbies. She writes, draws, plays the piano and dances. I have watched how one of her interests becomes overriding and all-consuming for a short period – and not long afterwards, it's playing second fiddle to another. (I always know which her favourite is, as I have to buy all the resources she needs to feed that interest!) She gets so consumed by her hobbies that she researches which new models, materials and machinery are available to enhance her skills. Although she is only ten, I cannot but admire her commitment. Do hold that thought for a minute.

The beauty of our universities is that they provide the perfect environment to start or develop an interest. The pressure of an average university environment – especially in most African countries, where classes are overcrowded, living conditions are often poor and students are constantly pressured to prepare for tests and examinations – makes developing a hobby of some sort significant for your survival (and that's putting it mildly).

Back to me for a moment. I was never good at sports (other than long-distance running), and my main interests were writing and politics. I was class and course representative a few times, and eventually became president of my departmental student association, the National Association of Zoology Students (NAZS). I wrote a lot of prose and poetry for fun, but I never made any effort to develop this. In fact, I never considered writing or politics as possible career directions. Fast forward to many years later, and I am involved in both. In terms of writing, *The Graduate Code* is my third book (I have also dabbled in songwriting and movie scriptwriting; I will talk about this in later chapters), and I am involved in politics as co-founder of Xn Foundation International (XnF), a UK-based and -registered non-governmental organisation (NGO) which supports African students in the diaspora. The foundation has convened the largest conference of Nigerian students in the UK for the last 11 years, and in that period we have achieved a huge amount (I will elaborate on this in Chapter 17). Someone asked me recently if I would be able to make a career out of either running XnF and/or writing, despite neither being connected with my undergraduate or postgraduate studies. In other words, if I stopped working as a consultant in environmental sustainability or education management (or as Mr Fix-it), could I have a career in supporting young people and in writing? I believe that I could.

Generally, people take different approaches to their hobbies, and some take them more seriously than others. These approaches are determined by how stressed people feel, the time they have available and sometimes even the environment they find themselves in. Some take a casual, low-key interest in their hobbies, while others take theirs to extremes. (One example of an interest often taken to the extreme, in African universities at least, is student unionism.) But one thing many students, graduates and working professionals fail to consider is that the hobby they enjoy could potentially be a career direction. Even more importantly, they never see their interest as developing skills or knowledge which could be relevant to their career success in future. A good way to appreciate this is by reading young African graduates' CVs (and I have reviewed quite a few!): virtually none mention their hobbies and activities as a core component of their skills and abilities. If they appear at all, they are shoved down to the bottom under the caption 'Hobbies', like an afterthought. They might well be sideline activities, but do they have to be?

I can honestly say that my current involvement and interest in supporting young people began way back during my undergraduate studies. Even though I had no idea how to develop this skill (and never considered it as a possible career route), it was ingrained in my personality, and blossomed under the right conditions. Just imagine what might have happened if I had carefully and consciously developed this skill. I was president of my university's student union for a year, but I never thought to include that in my CV. If I could go back and rewrite my first graduate CV, I would include the fact that this role helped me develop my people skills, problem-solving skills, fundraising skills, organisational skills, leadership skills… the list goes on.

There are many factors unique to hobbies, and three stand out for me. Number one is that most are easy to take up and practise; number two is that they help people to relax; and number three – the most important of all – is that with dedication, practice and the right resources and equipment they have the potential to develop into something more.

Many people begin their working life using the knowledge gained in their undergraduate and postgraduate studies and later decide to quit to follow their interests in a completely different role. I have noticed that such people do not necessarily prioritise their interests over the subject they studied because the financial reward is higher.

Instead, what these people have in common is job satisfaction. They have recognised the importance of spending time developing their hobbies and interests and turned them into a career.

I would like to emphasise here that even the most enjoyable jobs have their challenges and difficult days. Likewise, you may have a hobby at the moment that you love, but then tire of it in a few weeks', months' or years' time. I am not suggesting you should quit your studies and follow your hobby like your life depends on it. Instead, my advice is to place yourself in a position where you have options, and getting paid to do something you regard as a hobby is most definitely one of those.

Let's move on now to Activity 5, and take a look at what you do to relax.

. . . .

ACTIVITY 5

5a. What are your hobbies and interests?

5b. In order of priority, outline which of these have the potential to be developed into a career direction. Explain why you think this is the case.

5c. List the relevant skills and experiences that your current hobby(ies) or interest(s) has helped you develop and which could support a career route for the future.

NOTES

CHAPTER 6

Investing your time

. . . .

THE TENETS

6.1   The university is a great banking institution, and if
you invest your time under the right terms and conditions, you'll get great interest upon graduation.

6.2   Your time is the most important currency. Spend it wisely.

6.3   Spend time doing old but relevant things differently,
new career-enhancing things efficiently, and stop
doing career-defecting things totally.

6.4   There is always time, and even when there is none, you
can create it if it's important enough – for time management is the control of self in order to control time.

. . . .

This might sound a bit of a cliché, but investing your time (in the
sense of the Graduate Code) is like investing your money. You place
some funds in a fixed deposit in a bank account and agree the terms
of the investment at an agreed percentage over a period of time. At
the end of that time, you get your funds back, with value added. The
university is a great bank, and if you invest your time well, under the
right terms and conditions, you will get value after you graduate. It
may be a cliché, but like most clichés, it is also true.

The other saying I love is 'time is money'. Well, this one is definitely true – if you are anything like me as a student, being broke will be the norm. I can't remember ever having had cash that was not already accounted for. I never had spare cash and never used a bank. I'll tell you what I had in abundance, though: time. It was my currency, and if only I had known that back then, I would have acquired a lot more value for my career. Since I can't turn back the clock, I had better let you in on the 'time trick'.

Time is money means the creative use of time brings money. However, for some reason, graduates who have time don't seem to have money and those who have some money don't have enough time. These graduates have time at the 'wrong time'. For students, what they seem to have a lot of is time but not just that, they have time at the 'right time'.

The Graduate Code is all about encouraging people to take three principal steps: to develop skills differently if they are old but still relevant; to do new things efficiently if they are to enhance your career; and to stop doing things totally if they are irrelevant to your career. The most reliable resource you have, one which is much more precious than gold, is your time.

There is no time! There is no time! That is one of the biggest and most frequent lies I hear from the lips of students and professionals all over the world. I watch people express absolute wonder when I tell them what I do, and their first question is 'How do you find the time to do all these things?' Let's do a short time-mapping analysis to illustrate this.

The average first degree course in an African university lasts four years (or a minimum of five years for engineering and health-related programmes such as medicine, pharmacy, dentistry and optometry). There are generally two semesters per year, lasting three or four months each, including examination periods. The average person therefore spends about eight months studying – so every year there are four months unaccounted for. That's around 16–20 months of your undergraduate life.

Now, whether you are an average student or a super-serious book-grabbing and library-sleeping nerd, you would probably agree that even those four months are filled with a barrage of other course and non-course activities. The time you spend in clubs, society activities, student politics and mischievous rendezvous makes up a significant component of your graduate experiences, exposures and experimentations.

In my opinion (dare I say it?), the most time-consuming activity of all is social media. I did a quick analysis of how much time I spend on social media, and I was shocked to realise that on average I spend around two hours every day doing absolutely nothing. Actually, let me rephrase that. I can still function effectively without jeopardising my career and friendships if I don't spend that time on social media every day, despite needing to use it for work. If you spend a lot of time on social media, try asking yourself what you are doing on there for so long. Unless the answer is that you are looking for work, it might be good to get an idea of how much time you are spending (or perhaps wasting?). For me, there is nearly always time available, and even when it feels like there is none, you can create more if something is important enough.

I tried to think back to how I filled my time as an undergraduate, and I honestly could not remember. If I had done anything worthwhile with that time, I am sure I would remember what it was. There were certainly times spent in the library reading a lot, but this was mostly when examinations were round the corner. I also remember going to church, but that was probably no more than a couple of hours twice a week. Everything else about that time is hazy. I was not fortunate enough to own a phone or have access to the internet, and social media had not taken off at that time. At least not in my neck of the woods.

Since becoming a professional, I constantly struggle to find enough time. And judging by conversations with other professionals, this seems to be a common problem: there is a lot of time within the walls of higher education establishments and so little outside them. Obviously this is not literally the case; in universities, as everywhere else, there are the usual 24 hours in a day, 60 minutes in an hour and 60 seconds in a minute. The main issue is that you cannot slow time or speed it up, however hard you try. Instead, you need to learn to manage your time effectively. Time management is about aligning the demands on your time with your own needs. If you cannot effectively take control of your time while within those protected university walls, you will struggle in the outside world.

To help you learn to juggle the demands upon your time, there are loads of time management theories and models out there, many of which articulate the above ideas better than I ever could. For me, though, there are three fundamental steps to taking control of time.

Firstly, try understanding *what* you spend your time doing and *why* you spend your time doing those things.

Secondly, *prioritise* the things you do in order of how relevant they are to your overall success, both now and for your future career.

Thirdly, *adjust your activities* to give relevant subjects more time, minimise things irrelevant to your current and future career progress, and eliminate things that stand in the way of career success.

I realise that I have made these three steps sound very easy. However, this chapter is not intended to introduce time management from a theoretical perspective. Its main aim is to get you to think how your time could be spent more effectively. I cannot remember ever considering how to use my time more effectively or planning for the future during my undergraduate studies, even when I had a lot of time on my hands. Several young people in different African universities have told me that this aspect of student life has not changed.

Isn't it interesting, then, that those who have time worry less about planning and those who lack time worry more? If you flip this around, shouldn't those who have time be able to fit more in? I should point out here that when I am coming up to deadlines, my time management skills are often at their best, and so maybe I should introduce some sense of pressure to the equation.

The sense of pressure I just referred to is a cultural one. African culture is defined by social expectations and environmental pressures, which are associated in turn with time management. I'm sure most of you would agree that it is a lot more difficult to ask your parents for money after you have graduated than it was when you were at university. This is especially the case for middle- and low-income families, who I estimate make up more than 70% of parents of undergraduates at African universities. Children from high-income families tend for the most part to be sent overseas to study, so their situation is different.

Those who have already graduated will understand this cultural pressure a lot better. It is almost a taboo to be dependent on your parents after graduation. These are the parents who paid your tuition fees and provided most of what you needed while you were at university. There is a good chance you will end up living with your parents after graduating, even only temporarily while you figure things out, but I bet your bedroom will suddenly feel smaller. I know mine did, but why? I have a theory. You remember that pride your parents expressed while you were studying? That endless bragging to the neighbours and how they used every opportunity to slip in that phrase 'my daughter/son is at university'. Their glow of excitement when they woke up in the morning expecting to get a text about how your course was going. (When you eventually sent that text, it came with a request for more money.)

Do you also remember that silent cultural and even spiritual expectation that children will take care of their parents one day? Now you are about to graduate, do you feel that pressure building? Can you now understand why your room suddenly feels smaller? Why you feel like your parents are wondering why you still aren't working after graduation and helping with the bills? You may feel helpless and angry when it seems impossible to get a job, however much effort you make. You may feel like you are endlessly being asked to submit CVs for endless job opportunities that never materialise. Do you feel the pressure building? And after all that effort you eventually get a job, but you may well have to travel endless hours in endless traffic pitching to endless customers with endless excuses. You spend that salary of yours even before you get paid, so you are endlessly living in deficit. And even if you are one of the lucky ones who have a well-paid job, you may well have to jeopardise your happiness and your family's happiness to ensure that life goes on.

You may wonder why I have painted such a grim picture here to emphasise the pressure after graduation. So let me explain.

There are two particular times when my time management capacity is super-efficient. Firstly, when I am under pressure, and secondly, when I am enjoying what I am doing. If I had known the pressures I would face after graduating, I would have brought those pressures forward to enhance my time management skills while still at university. Then I would have spent my time doing things I loved that would also enhance my abilities to face this post-graduation pressure. Since I can't go back to that time, I won't dwell on it, but you can see why it is so important to recognise how much time you have and why you need to make time for relevant activities while at university.

This takes me on to Activity 6. The aim of this activity is to get you to think more carefully about which activities consume your time but have few or no career-enhancing properties. (It is possible, of course, that you haven't figured out yet how some of these activities could enhance your future career, and that is also fine.)

ACTIVITY 6

6a. List the six key activities that consume the majority of your daily time as a student, graduate or young professional.

6b. Allocate estimated hours to these six key activities and then label them in order of career relevance (0 for no career relevance; 1 for little career relevance and 2 for great career relevance). If you are spending a lot of time on activities not relevant to your career, is there any way you could reorganise your day to change this? You may find it helpful to refer back to your answers to Activity 4a to give you a clear perspective here.

NOTES

CHAPTER 7

Creating your curriculum vitae (CV)

· ·

THE TENETS

7.1   The best time to write a CV is when you're not actually looking for a job, because it's the basis for your connections and the introduction of your personality and capacity.

7.2   All the standard sections of a CV can be filled up before or after graduation, even if you have no paid work – provided you know what to do, how to do it and when to do it.

7.3   Aim for a two-page CV that tries to condense ten pages' worth of content instead of a two-page CV that tries to extend half a page of content.

· ·

So I was addressing a group of about 120 students recently. Midway through my talk, I asked them, 'How many of you have written a CV?' I could see them looking really confused. Why? Because they didn't understand why I had asked the question. They were in their penultimate year of university and had an extra year of studies to get through before they graduated. They didn't see the point of writing a CV when they weren't applying for jobs. However, over time I have come to realise that this is actually the best time to write a CV.

Writing your CV before you start looking for work gives you two advantages: firstly, it shows you what you still need to do to get the job you want; and secondly, it gives you the impetus to do the right things to shape your CV to your future career. Most CVs include these main sections:

- Personal details (name, address, email, social media handles)
- Education (including professional training and short courses taken)
- Work experience and skills acquired (starting with the most recent)
- Membership of professional bodies and affiliations
- Awards and publications (including awarding bodies and dates)
- Hobbies and interests
- References (personal, academic and professional).

These sections form the bedrock of how your CV is presented, and give a brief and well-articulated overview of your qualifications, experiences and capacities. Getting the content right is vital.

I have seen and reviewed more than a thousand graduate CVs in the last ten years, and it has been a fascinating experience. During this time, I have rarely seen one longer than three pages. These have not been intentionally short; they have simply lacked enough content. (To be honest, most three-page CVs come from superstar graduates who have spent their time at university effectively and kept themselves busy.) By the time you have included the most basic sections – your personal information, education, hobbies/interests and references – what else can you write?

Unless you invent things or pluck skills from outer space to fill up your CV, it can be hard to stretch it to two pages. Even if you increase the font size and line spacing to fill those two pages, your CV will still contain the same information. It might look okay if it's all you have, but is it all you need? Let me reframe that with an even better, more probing question: 'Is that *all* you can do?' Take a look again at the standard CV sections above. They can all be filled during your undergraduate studies if you know *what* to do, *how* to do it and *when* to do it.

Just for clarity, I do have a short version of my CV, as most international research grant proposals require principal and co-investigators on the grant to submit a two-page CV for positive assessments. However, there is a huge difference between a two-page CV that condenses ten pages' worth of content and a two-page CV that tries to expand half a page of content.

I mentioned earlier that I spent a brief period in employment after graduating, but allow me to tell you the story of how I got that job with the help of the first ever professional CV I wrote and submitted.

After my first degree, I went on to do my master's degree and then my doctorate. The only professional work I had ever done was during my national service at Platinum Bank (which I talked about in Chapter 4), and I had been a full-time student the rest of the time. My PhD supervisor had met a Vice President (VP) of BG Group – one of the world's largest oil and gas firms – on a work trip, they had spoken about BG Group's Nigerian branch operations, and my name had come up. Upon my supervisor's return, he handed me the VP's business card and I dropped him an email along with my CV. It was my first ever professionally written CV, despite never having had what you could call a profession before. I was just a nerdy bookworm. Anyway, he invited me over to BG Group's head office in Reading, UK, for a chat. I remember being on the train from Lancaster and wondering what this chat would be about. As it turned out, the chat turned into a job offer for the role of local content adviser for their new Nigerian branch operation. I returned to Lancaster, and a week later got a call confirming my pay offer. I nearly collapsed when the lady on the phone told me they were offering me £500 per day. For a student who was just wrapping up his PhD and had never done any main professional work, that was overwhelming.

Let me put that comment in perspective.

Up until then, my only work in the UK had been three part-time jobs between studies – working as a pot washer in a kitchen, a cleaner in a local market and a care assistant in an elderly people's home. Even though this was manual vocational work, I still picked up important skills that became part of me, even though these were not represented on my CV at the time.

I imagine you're wondering why a globally reputable firm would offer a high-level advisory role to a student who had no prior professional experience. I'll tell you: the CV I sent the VP was ten pages long. No doubt you're now wondering how I could possibly have had a ten-page CV. The answer to that is that every section of my CV was full of relevant information even though I was still a student. I had written this CV three years after graduation from my first degree; if I could fill these sections despite starting late, imagine the opportunities you will have to enhance your CV if you start immediately.

Generally, your CV is the basis for making professional connections and introducing employers to your personality and capacity. And whether you plan to go into employment, start your own enterprise or go into further education, you always need a CV. Currently, I have four different CVs for different purposes, but these have taken a long time to put together. I have one for my consultancy career; one for my arts, creative media and writing side gig; one focusing on my passion for charity work and work in female empowerment; and a final CV focusing on my education and youth development sideline. (There is a fifth one, actually, which condenses the other four and acts as 'Akan's one-stop shop'.)

Since we have already discussed thinking about different career directions, it makes sense to also consider developing different CVs alongside your different career options. CVs are 'living documents' and need to be updated regularly, so make it a point of duty to update your CV at least once every six months – whether you are a student, graduate or young professional.

Keeping in mind all that I've told you in this chapter, let's move on to Activity 7 and think about how your CV might look.

· ·

ACTIVITY 7

7a.   Try writing a two-page CV. Let's see what you come up with.

7b.   Which sections of your CV do you think need a facelift? What can you do to improve them before you update this CV in six months' time?

NOTES

NOTES

CHAPTER 8

Working for no pay

. . . .

THE TENETS

8.1 If work experience is crucial for graduate employment, then volunteering is essential for skills development and career enjoyment.

8.2 It is bad if you don't have relevant skills; worse if you have skills and don't know that you do, and worst if you don't have skills, don't know that you need them and so do not develop them.

8.3 Try to develop skills through working for no pay so that in future you'll enjoy the thrills of working for pay.

8.4 You can't live, study or work within or around a university, the biggest provider of employment, and not be exposed to working. It makes no sense!

. . . .

If there are things you need to buy to make your life better, why would you want to work for no pay? When there is pressure from every direction, why would you consider it? When parents, family and other loved ones are depending on you, what is the advantage? Why would working for free be a fundamental component of the Graduate Code? My answer is simple. What you might call working for no pay is also known as volunteering, provided it is intentional and with a clear objective.

I had never heard this term in Nigeria during my studies or early professional career, and only came across it when I began studying in the UK for my master's degree. Even then, it seemed like an alien concept.

Over the years, I have had many conversations with young graduates about their job-seeking experiences, and one thing keeps coming up: the biggest challenge they face is their lack of work experience. In their CVs, they have the key sections written up, as discussed in Chapter 7, but struggle to write anything in the work experience section. This puts recruiters in a difficult position when trying to decide whether to employ you, don't you think?

The employers I have spoken with want someone who can fulfil the job requirements, and they need evidence of this before considering hiring you. A good way to demonstrate this is through volunteer work in a similar role.

Don't get me wrong here; employees often need further training. But why would a company choose to recruit someone who needed substantial amounts of training if there was someone else applying who had the relevant skills and knowledge? Generally, employers have some sort of induction process for new starters, but that is all it is – induction. It exposes you to the workplace culture, job expectations and environmental dynamics that are peculiar to that organisation. But inductions do not show you how to do the job itself.

The disconnect between what is studied at university and what is expected in the workplace highlights the need for employers to have a series of training schemes for young employees. Most graduates just do not have the right skills for employment. In fact, they do not have any form of work experience. But if work experience is crucial to ensure employment after graduation (and we've seen that it is), shouldn't you always seek out relevant volunteering experiences during your time as an undergraduate or even while you are a professional if it allows you to pick up the key skills you most desperately need?

Of course, volunteering has to be intentional and strategic. The art of volunteering is to use it as a basis for getting the work experience you need and would not be able to get otherwise. I am not saying that you only have to volunteer for the sake of picking up new relevant experiences, because you can volunteer – and probably should – for causes that mean a lot to you and the betterment of society. But within the context of the Graduate Code, let's stick with skills and work experience if we may. As well as work experience, you will also pick up valuable knowledge and skills. Someone asked me recently if volunteering was even a thing in Africa. It had better become a thing, I thought, or students will continue to struggle after they graduate.

You may be wondering if employers value skills gained through unpaid work. Well, I have not yet seen a CV which lists someone's pay alongside their listed work experiences. What a CV captures (and rightly so) is the knowledge gained and skills acquired as a result of relevant work experience. The question of pay will only come up if you are being seriously considered with a role – it is your CV which gets you through the door, by showing you have the skills to do the job in the first place. So let's focus on that for a minute.

What sort of skills do employers generally look for? This partly depends on the job you want to do, but there are five key skills which apply to most roles: presentation, people management, problem solving, project management and public speaking. Note that these are not exhaustive, but I need to use them to make a clear point. Let's call them the 5Ps.

The 5Ps have nothing to do with your programme of study. Even though I graduated with first-class honours, I didn't have any of these listed skills after finishing my first degree. (If I did have any of these skills, then I didn't realise I did or consider them important enough to want to develop them further to prepare for life after graduation. That tells you something, don't you think?)

It is not ideal if you don't have these skills at all, but at least you know employers are looking for them. It is equally bad (or possibly worse) if you do have these skills but are unaware of it or unwilling to develop them. Worst of all is if you don't have any of the 5Ps, aren't aware you need them and have no idea how to develop them.

Taking presentation as an example, I remember that the only presentation I gave during my studies was on the mandatory seminar we had to deliver in our final year. (I did give a few public speeches as a student politician, but I never realised how relevant these skills were until many years down the line.) Now I regularly prepare and deliver PowerPoint presentations, but it took a long time to hone this skill, which I need in my professional work as a consultant and trainer.

People management as a skill is a fundamental one to master, because professional work environments are made up of different people, some of whom can be challenging to deal with. Back in my undergraduate days, I was president of my student union and had to manage an executive team while delivering a list of activities in the department. Not until recently did I consider that it was the first building block of my people management skills. Now I fundamentally rely on this skill to develop and management strategic partnerships between international organisations.

For project management and problem solving, I was totally clueless until I got thrown into the deep end with a master's degree research project, and oh! how I struggled. Imagine if I had started developing these skills when I had time, or if I had created the time to do so. Now I need to be able to manage projects and solve complex problems, or else I'm lost.

The first thing to note is that your course of study doesn't impart these skills to you –you need to get creative. The best way to start the process of gaining the 5Ps (and other relevant skills) is to develop these skills through volunteer work so that in the future you enjoy the thrill of being paid to work.

I have spoken a lot about the value of volunteering in bridging the skills gap needed for employment, but does that mean that if you intend to start your own enterprise or undertake further education, you do not need to volunteer? Absolutely not. The skills you pick up are always relevant, whether you go into employment, enterprise or further education.

In Chapter 6, we looked at how much of your time can be consumed by activities irrelevant to your future career, and, with that in mind, it makes sense to show you how to be creative in developing a volunteer plan and making it happen.

I was first exposed to the fundamentals and opportunities offered by volunteering while studying and living in the UK, and so it was natural to believe that it was unrealistic to expect these in Africa. And (or so I thought), even if you did expect to volunteer somewhere, this experience would only be relevant in the professional world where NGOs and corporate organisations reign, and not within a university. Oh, how wrong I was. The potential for volunteering is universal, even though your environment and culture dictate the type of volunteer opportunities available.

First, let me paint you a series of pictures of how to create volunteering opportunities for yourself. It is important to note that every example here is real and has been tested.

How many companies do you think are within or close to your university? How many small shops and private enterprises are there? If you don't know, you might want to find out.

To get an idea of these figures, I looked at fifteen universities in six different African countries, and I estimate that the average number of small firms and shops was 150 within a one-kilometre radius. I've given you an average figure because I visited some really small universities too, but for the average public university, the numbers are huge – a friend confirmed that one public university in Kenya had in excess of 300 companies, small firms and shops within and surrounding it. There is a good reason why universities attract businesses: suppliers of goods and services have a ready population of students and staff, often multicultural in nature, to feed their existence.

Every university is also a client to a myriad of business contractors and service providers, so maybe that could be your entry point. You have probably heard the term 'university town' to refer to somewhere that thrives fundamentally because of the presence of a university. Lancaster, UK, where I live, is such a town. It would probably survive without a university, but you need to see for yourself how quiet it gets at Easter, summer and Christmas, when most students return home for the holidays.

Now with 150 potential enterprises within and around your university, you have 150 potential volunteering locations. How might you do this, you ask? Well, this is how. You write up your CV, get references from someone credible – such as your parents, guardian or lecturer – dress up nicely, go to one of these firms or shops, present your CV and the references and ask if you could work, assist, support or just learn from their staff for a few hours a week on a volunteer basis. If you never try, you'll never know. (I did try this, so I do know.) Do you know how many hours you spend doing absolutely nothing in a week? Well, how about diverting that time into gaining some experience instead?

Let's consider another possible volunteering opportunity. Over a six-month period, I visited about twenty universities in different African countries, and on each university campus, I noticed the huge number of posters, flyers and signboards for different daily events, programmes or activities. It can seem overwhelming, and with the huge amount of activities available on campus, you may wonder what you should do. The key here is to investigate what's on offer: find out who is in charge of planning which events, when they take place, and how they go about organising them. Prepare yourself as you would if you were approaching a business for volunteer work, get some references if you must, and ask to support or be part of the team planning the event. (There's a small chance they might offer to pay you for this, but be open to volunteering your time for free.)

Anyway, let's move on to considering another volunteer opportunity now. Have you noticed that a university is actually a professional workplace? It might not seem so to you as a student, because you tend to shuffle between your chalet, classrooms, cafeterias and clubs – the four Big Cs (components) of student life – sleeping, reading, eating and playing. There is one Big C that is missing, though, which I think most students lack. I'd like to call this the Creative Zone – where everything outside the usual, mundane and traditional thrives. In fact, it is in this space that the Graduate Code exists. A balanced and progressive student life should include five Big Cs: sleeping, reading, eating, playing and creating.

Back to my point about universities being professional workplaces, though.

A university is usually the biggest employer in your jurisdiction. The University of Benin in Nigeria employs in excess of 6,000 staff members and the University of Copperbelt in Zambia employs in excess of 1,000 staff. With this in mind, help me with this for a minute. It doesn't make sense to live and study within the walls of the biggest local employer for three or four years and not be exposed to working culture. You need to consider crossing the student–staff divide to learn about work. The first ever volunteer work I did (even though I didn't know it was volunteering at the time) was helping a busy professor in my department manage his diary – almost like the role of a personal assistant. This was the same professor who inspired my passion for environmental management.

So what should you do? Prepare your CV, get references, approach an administrator, a lecturer, a director, an officer and ask, 'Please can I volunteer to work for you or your department for a few hours a week supporting events/preparing documents/cleaning the office/ learning lecture planning/planning departmental meetings/liaising with students on your behalf…?' The list is endless. (And as above, if they offer to pay you for your time, that's an unexpected but welcome bonus!)

There is a volunteer opportunity that seems to appeal readily to students, and that is within the realms of student politics and religious organisations. For this one, many will go all out to campaign, step on a few toes just to get elected and spend endless hours managing a religious organisation during their studies. In Africa, student politics and religion are a big deal. But how many students actually see student unionism or involvement in a religious organisation's activities as a career enhancer? At times student unionism can become a platform for stirring up crises and arguments and selfishly grasping at temporary power, although true and selfless student unionism also exists. (After all, '*Aluta continua, Victoria ascerta*'.) Religious organisations are well structured to give meaning and value to student living, which is positive in itself, but do you remember the 5Ps? Student unionism and participation in religious organisations have the potential to help you develop all of those skills – and much more – if done creatively. In the UK, for instance, student unions are run like a professional outfit with laid-down precepts, regulations and even paid leave, and those who volunteer do so under clear rules of engagement. (Could student unionism in Africa be better structured? That's another discussion in itself, but the point remains that you need to see, seek and steal every opportunity to enhance your skills for a future graduate career.) And yes, I do mean 'stealing', because if you don't grab the chance, someone else will.

Even for those planning to study further after graduation, volunteering at university is a great way to learn about postgraduate studies. Where better to learn about the skills and preparation needed for further studies than within the walls of a university? So think about getting a master's degree or PhD student as a mentor and learn the one true experience that makes further education different from undergraduate studies – which is independence and management. (I will come back to this in Chapters 15 and 20.)

On a final note, I can hear some sceptics among you muttering, 'What if none of these volunteer opportunities exist? What do I do then?' Well, I have only one answer for you – create one. How can you do this? Stick with me, and you'll find out.

Let's move on to Activity 8 now, and think about how you could enhance your own skills through volunteering.

. . . .

ACTIVITY 8

8a. Without mentioning the 5Ps listed earlier in this chapter, state five other general skills that might be useful to an employer.

8b. If you could volunteer right now, what three skills would you want to develop further, and why?

8c. If you were to start volunteering, what kind of volunteering opportunities would you take on, and how would you go about making this happen? (It would be useful here to keep your answers to 8b in mind.)

CHAPTER 9

Learning with no box

· ·

THE TENETS

9.1 Thinking outside the box is good, but thinking with no box is better, because for creativity to thrive, captivity must die.

9.2 Learning for examinations and reports is good, but learning for graduation and profession is even better, so don't conform when you should reform, or you'll become a graduate with no form.

9.3 Learn your course content in isolation to become a graduate, but learn in relation to a career context to become a true professional.

9.4 Spending time getting better at something you do like while studying a course you don't like could make the difference between a painfully confusing graduate career and a happy eventful one.

· ·

I'm sure you know the expression 'think outside the box', which I like to see as alluding to the fact that for creativity to thrive, captivity must die. The 'box' in this case is society's hold on you to conform when you need to reform, which results in graduates with no form.

(Okay, I digress; I am getting carried away with rhymes here.) Some people take the expression a step further and advise you to 'think with no box'. I would advise you to take this to heart, and to 'learn with no box'.

The way universities are set up automatically restricts you in some sense, and this affects the courses you choose and, by implication, your career direction. When you have studied a course for four or five years, you are expected to know everything about your subject. (This isn't necessarily the case, though; many African universities encourage students to learn to pass examinations and not to prepare them for graduation and professional life.)

If you only learn information to pass examinations, after you graduate that knowledge tends to become irrelevant 'luggage' in your brain that you can't wait to offload. Semester after semester, you cram in information and parrot it back as you progress to the following year. I remember in the first few months of my master's degree in the UK, I felt incompetent and a fraud even though I had graduated with a first-class honours degree. I realised then that the examination-only format of learning in Nigeria had stopped me retaining knowledge. My chronic dependence on the lecturers and administrators of that knowledge had made my supposedly curious mind lazy and unproductive. From a conversation I had with a few professors recently, it seems that fifteen years down the line, things have not changed. Against this background, you have a huge opportunity to differentiate yourself.

Generally, I would say the majority of a student's learning is the course content rather than putting that learning into a career context. When I studied zoology, I learnt a lot about parasitology, entomology, hydrobiology, histology and several other 'ologies'. The trouble was that I learnt all this information in isolation, whereas learning needs to be in relation to life after graduation if it is to enhance your career. So my first lesson, as I alluded to in Chapter 8, is to understand your course in relation to your future career.

To differentiate yourself from other graduates seeking work, it is fundamental to learn outside the boundaries of your actual course of study. I remember saying this at a forum and the students acted like I had said something sacrilegious, but let me use three real-life cases to show you why this is so important. Firstly, if you are training to be a lawyer, learn about something different, for example sustainable agriculture. Secondly, if you are training to be a business management graduate, try learning something highly scientific, such as energy efficiency in sustainable housing. And thirdly, if you are a chemistry student, learn something about business development. Teaching at universities tends to be compartmentalised, so you need to make the effort to 'learn outside the box'.

In my first example, a trainee lawyer who has spent time learning about sustainable agriculture would potentially be better placed for employment after graduation than their contemporaries. Africa is currently in an era where agriculture is taking centre stage. One of the African Development Bank's main strategies is 'Feed Africa', and governments across the continent are increasing their focus on reducing importation and increasing production of the food we eat. Sustainable agriculture is about efficient supply chains and strategic partnerships, and effective legal frameworks to support these collaborations are invaluable. And that is where the lawyer who has studied agriculture is differentiated from other law graduates. Traditionally, law and agriculture are seen as two distinct faculties, but by taking deliberate action to combine the two you can vastly improve your future employability.

For my second example I suggested that a business graduate would do well to arm themselves with a sound knowledge of energy efficiency. With over 600 million Africans in dire need of electricity against a backdrop of an energy security crisis, a business graduate could make a fortune right now by setting up and running an energy-efficiency consulting firm. Such a graduate could also find work in the business department of an energy company or in the energy department of a business management consultancy. The more you know, the more options you have.

My third example concerned a chemistry student learning about business development. Do you know how many different organisations need chemists? A vast amount: pharmaceutical companies, breweries, fertiliser production outfits, food and drink producers... the list goes on. In fact, many people who rise to the top of their profession and lead huge organisations such as these are either business professionals with a science head or average scientists with an MBA.

I am not saying here that all lawyers should learn about agriculture or that all chemists should learn about business, though. But if you want to stand out from other graduates, you do need to consciously learn about another subject outside your course of study. It is even better if the other subject is something you enjoy or have an aptitude for. You remember that group of 200 students I mentioned in Chapter 2, half of whom disliked the course they were studying at university? Imagine if those students had decided to learn about something they enjoyed alongside the course they had registered for. The only difference would be that they wouldn't have the same pressures to take lecture notes, study handouts or sit examinations. And because they would be motivated to learn more about the other subject, they would remember more about it than what they were expected to parrot back in end-of-year examinations.

But do universities allow students to attend lectures for other courses?

I asked many different African professors if it would upset them if an unregistered student attended their classes, and I got a variety of responses. Some said they would not be offended at all, provided the student didn't sit any examinations. (Little did they know that this hypothetical student would have no intention of trying to sit exams.) Some said they would prefer the student to explain to them why they were not registered for that course but wished to sit in on the lectures, but ultimately, if the explanation made sense, they would allow it. One professor said sarcastically that they barely know all the students in the class anyway until they have to mark their examination sheets, so students can do whatever they please. A few professors gave very interesting responses, and this made it for me. These professors said that such a student would be their star learner and that they would take that student more to heart. When I asked why, their response was that this would be a 'true student', one who really and truly wanted to learn about the subject matter and wasn't there because they felt forced to stay. Now isn't that something?

Taking this idea further, I began to investigate different university policies and regulations in various African countries. I wanted to find out if any university regulations prevented a student from attending a course they hadn't registered for and which was unrelated to their actual programme of study. Surprisingly, there weren't any such rules at the universities I investigated. Some prevented students taking examinations in a course outside their main programme of study, which creates a conflict. By implication, the university system restricts you from 'learning with no box', but in practice legally permits it. Being aware of this can totally change your perception.

If I may, I'd like to tell you a little more about myself to illustrate this.

Midway through my PhD, I realised I didn't really like science laboratory work. Like many others, I was one of those students who started a PhD for all the wrong reasons. I had just concluded my master's degree in the UK, I didn't have a job, and I was due to return to Nigeria. The decision to do a doctorate degree was impulsive, to say the least. I frantically started applying to different UK universities and searching for a scholarship at the same time. I'm sure you know how hard it can be to self-fund a one-year master's degree, but paying for a three-year PhD would swallow you up. I was blessed and got a call for an interview from Lancaster University while still writing up my master's dissertation at the University of Wales, Aberystwyth, and it was the call that changed my life. I admit it was desperation that led me to start my PhD, but I soon realised its potential for transformation.

My PhD was on the effects of pesticides on non-target species, meaning earthworms, enchytraeids and collembola. ('Creepy crawlies', in other words.) So basically I was a laboratory-based research student. I really struggled, I must tell you, but only because I didn't have a flair for laboratory work. So to take the edge off, I also focused on things I really enjoyed, and this involved 'learning with no box'. The UK educational system allows for this, but the only trouble was that my supervisors really wanted me to complete the PhD despite these distractions. During my science-based PhD in environmental management, I wrote and published a book of poetry, and completed business management and enterprise fellowship programmes at Cambridge University in the UK and Stanford University in the US. I won several awards for my writing and non-PhD associated work, including the British Council International Student of the Year 2006, an award for which more than two thousand people applied. This was the beginning of my consulting career combining sustainability and business, and is what I do now.

I would like to think that 'learning with no box' during your undergraduate studies is a precursor to a postgraduate education later. It is like saying you began your master's degree earlier. Think about that for a minute. Most postgraduate studies involve specialising in a particular topic within a broader subject. The term 'master's' implies your expertise in that topic.

Generally, people who go on to do a master's degree usually pick an area they are interested in. It might be something they studied as part of the undergraduate degree they didn't like, or a new area of interest they have developed as a result of volunteering or studying something outside the box. (If a student completes an undergraduate degree they dislike and then decides to do a master's degree in exactly the same subject, I would recommend they see a doctor.) Focusing on that extra learning while studying for your undergraduate programme is similar to starting a master's degree early.

I would argue the same for hobbies and interests. Remember Chapter 5, 'Getting paid for your hobbies'? If you can invest some time learning about other interesting and potentially career-enhancing subjects to expand your knowledge base, doesn't it also make sense to learn how to improve on your interests? Take my brother-in-law as an example. He taught himself to draw comic book art when he was at secondary school. When he was at university, he developed his hobby further and read lots of books to teach himself how to draw for 3D animations, even though his undergraduate degree was in mechanical engineering. The skills and knowledge he has acquired are in high demand in Africa, and now he is planning a career in animation.

Some people are dismissive of their hobbies, saying they're just something they do for relaxation and didn't have to learn. That may be the case, but you can always improve your skills if you put more time in. There are e-books, short free online courses and endless YouTube videos on almost everything. So while you are studying that course you don't really enjoy, spend some time getting better at something you *do* enjoy. It could be the difference between a painfully confusing graduate career and a happy eventful one.

This takes me to the big question: now that you know the significance of learning with no box, how do you go about learning this way? Well, here are a few pointers.

Firstly, go and take some classes in another department you are interested in. It might feel strange at first, but could differentiate you from other graduates after your course finishes. (Please make sure you find out what works best in your university before you do this – I don't want you getting into trouble and blaming me and *The Graduate Code* for it!)

Secondly, make friends with people at university in different departments, particularly if they are studying subjects which interest you. Add an extra layer to the 'friend mix' to increase the number of people you interact with in the area which interests you. It is all too easy to get into the habit of hanging out with old school friends or friends from your own programme.

The internet is also a good place to start. You can find information on just about anything, and there are huge amounts of short free online courses available. Instead of spending your expensive data allowance reading about which celebrity bought the latest designer dress, take a new short course every month. Afterwards, seek to use this new knowledge whenever you can. Then you can buy a designer dress when you earn (if that is your thing).

Interestingly, I remember doing something during my undergraduate years which has now become the bedrock of what I do professionally. Every semester, I would look for a student in my class who hadn't done well academically the previous year or someone who was struggling with the course. I would ask this student to be my reading partner, putting added pressure on me to learn enough to be able to explain the course to them. As naive as I was, I knew that if I learnt something well enough to teach it, then I would truly understand it. I soon became addicted to the feeling that I was doing something of value. This is why everything I do today, including writing this book, is driven by the need to build my professional and personal capacity and to have an impact on people. Can you identify what drives you?

Let's move on to Activity 9 now, and consider some possible ways *you* could 'learn outside the box'.

. . . .

ACTIVITY 9

9a. If you could choose to learn about a new subject, list three subjects outside your current or past course of study that you would enjoy learning more about.

9b. Is there a relationship between these subjects and the course you are currently studying (or which you studied)? If yes, how does each of them relate to your course?

9c. List two possible career options that could combine the knowledge from your current course of study (or which you studied) and the knowledge from the extra learning outside your main course of study.

9d. List the ways you will ensure that you 'learn with no box'. Tell me how you intend to do this over the next three to six months.

CHAPTER 10

Finding a mentor

. . . .

THE TENETS

10.1 Get a mentor to navigate between the town and the gown and to bridge the gaps between academia and industry.

10.2 While some pitfalls are crucial to your professional development, others are difficult to move beyond. Having a mentor can help you avoid major pitfalls and lead to professional success.

10.3 Every education course and career direction has its peculiarities; mentors are crucial to sharpen your adaptability.

10.4 To get what you need from a mentor, you need to know who you are, remember what you do, understand what you need, appreciate who they are and learn from what they do.

. . . .

Over two years ago, I started writing a blog of my experiences when travelling all over Africa doing consultation, advisory and facilitation work in government policy, business strategy and capacity building. I mainly post my entries on LinkedIn and

Instagram, my favourite social media platforms. This activity began as a way to while away time, but it has progressed into capturing trends around the challenges and opportunities in different African countries.

My blog is written in a motivational style, and I have noticed an interesting trend over the last year. More than 60% of the emails and direct messages I have received via these social media platforms have been requests from all kinds of individuals wanting me to mentor them. But I have also noticed that over 70% of these requests have come from working professionals. I find this rather intriguing – I expected most working professionals to have figured out their career direction by that stage in their lives. The fact that I was wrong suggests that if people need mentoring when they are working professionals, students and young graduates probably have a greater need for mentoring. In fact, everyone needs some form of mentoring. (I still get mentored even now. That reminds me! Go back and read the Foreword of this book, because two of my mentors wrote it together. How cool is that?)

Who is a mentor? And what does it mean to mentor? The *Oxford English Dictionary* defines a mentor as 'an experienced and trusted adviser' and 'to mentor' as 'to advise or train'. A mentor mentors a mentee, or protégé (i.e. you). There are different kinds of mentors depending on what advice or training you desire. There are life mentors, marriage mentors, project mentors, and the list goes on. What you need is a career mentor! And in some sense, *The Graduate Code* is a career mentor in book form, especially as every chapter of perspectives and advice is followed by a series of instructions and activities for the reader.

The vision statements and governance strategies of many universities describe them as establishments aiming to improve knowledge, create value and bridge the gaps between 'town and gown'. 'Gown' alludes to the glorious graduation gown and depicts the intellectuality and knowledge base of the university environment. 'Town' alludes to the non-academic community that a university interacts with and depicts the influence on society of the university's proficiency in knowledge and research.

As I have mentioned before, there is a clear disconnect between academia and industry, and it is the student or graduate's responsibility to bridge this gap if no one else will. Students and young graduates have access to teachers and lecturers who provide them with the necessary knowledge to enhance the 'gown' dimension of the university offer. What they lack are those who provide the 'town' dimension. Might this be the role of a mentor? Or could your lecturer also perform that role? I have asked this question in different student forums, and the responses have been pretty discouraging to say the least: 'How can my lecturer be a mentor when they are totally unapproachable?' 'How can my lecturer be a mentor when they are socially unavailable though academically present? What is the point of a mentor when you cannot engage them to get the advice and guidance you truly need? I can't see the point of that.' You might consider them role models, but mentors? Absolutely not.

The term 'role model' is generally used to refer to an individual whose behaviour, success and examples can be emulated or copied by others, especially by younger people. Role models are influencers and individuals in positions of social authority who are mostly far removed from their admirers. You may see your parents as role models, but how much influence do they have on your career? And yes, good parents make great life mentors, but do they make good career mentors? Unless they have experience of working in your chosen career, I struggle to see how they could guide you appropriately.

So while I advocate for everyone to have great role models, I am an even greater advocate of you striving to be a role model yourself.

To help you become that person, why reinvent the wheel when many others have trodden the path you are now on?

For me, having career mentors should be non-negotiable, especially at the stage of deciding the direction you want your career to take. Students, young graduates and working professionals need career mentors if they are to avoid pitfalls and have a successful professional life. Some believe that these pitfalls are crucial in moulding you as a person, but there are pits and there are PITS, and some are too deep to climb out of.

There are many theories and career guidance books available, and while some are good, others are truly exceptional. But one thing that many young professionals have told me is that such books always seem to lack local relevance and cultural adaptability. This book is intended to be an exception to that rule: while it is still a career guide, it is based on personal experiences and infused with Africanness. However, this book alone is not enough; different subject matters and career directions have different peculiarities associated with them and mentors are crucial to help you align your studies with your career direction.

Let me give you a couple of examples I have observed by interacting with different graduates and professionals over the years. These are perhaps specific to Africa, so stick with me on this. Take medical doctors, for instance. They go into practice for a while after six years in university education, and then they undertake a master's degree in public health. At present there is a huge demand for public health professionals, and pure medicine does not cover topics like the increasing availability of public health grants and funding and the societal challenges and opportunities associated with public health. So there is a clear advantage in doing an extra public health programme after studying medicine.

I have also heard advice that you should not do a Master of Business Administration (MBA) unless you have some professional experience in business and management. If you lack experience, its relevance and usability will not be understood. Top business schools include professional business and management experience as a criterion for admission. A career mentor in your field would know this.

It is important not to confuse the role of a mentor with that of a trainer/teacher or a coach, as these terms are often (and incorrectly) used to mean the same thing. Specifically, I need to clarify these so that I can highlight why I prefer to recommend finding a mentor rather than a trainer or a coach. Trainers and coaches often have a role to play in career development, but they do not take the place of mentors.

I think it's best if I clarify here what each of these roles involves. A trainer imparts knowledge and information and backs it up with clear instructions and explanations, while a coach enhances the use of knowledge by setting tasks and monitoring performance. A mentor, on the other hand, enhances your capability and self-reliance. A trainer teaches you over a relatively short period of time, which normally ends after you have been given the relevant knowledge (or in the case of coaching, after a task has been completed). On the contrary, a relationship with a mentor is long-term, with no particular end date.

While a trainer or coach is likely to set you goals and targets and to support you in achieving them, a mentor will encourage you to set your own goals and then support you in achieving them. With a trainer or coach, you are not in control, but with a mentor you are in charge of your career destiny. Being trained and being mentored are very different things, although a mentor may advise you to undergo training or coaching (or even train you themselves) at certain points in your career development if that is what is required.

Due to the nature and significance of being mentored, you cannot afford to pick just anyone. You need guidance and clarity. To buddy up with a mentor, you need to know who you are, remember what you do, understand what you need, appreciate who they are and learn from what they do. Anyone successful and experienced enough to mentor you will usually have a clear idea of what makes them tick. Mentors also need mentors, and unlike coaches and trainers, they also want to learn more and get better at what they do. Seek a mentor who you can also help and support where required. Figure out what interests them and what sort of support they need, so you can offer them a mutually beneficial relationship when you approach them. Many people make the mistake of only offering a one-sided relationship. For a mentor who is busy – and most are – there is no pull for them to engage with you and no basis for a continuous relationship.

In a world that is changing fast, avoid thinking of a mentor in traditional terms. A mentor does not necessarily need to be older, have more qualifications or more experience than you. A mentor should be someone whose philosophies are similar to yours, someone who challenges you, and someone who has more experience than you in the area you wish to improve yourself in but is also able to motivate you to explore other areas of interest. Your ultimate goal is to get the career advice from them you need, and becoming their buddy is a consequence of that engagement. Spread your net to find the mentor fit for you. Use the internet, read articles, contact your university's alumni office, use social media platforms, and get yourself that mentor who will be your career accelerator.

Let's move on now to Activity 10, and consider your role models and what you would do if you had a mentor.

ACTIVITY 10

10a. Who are your role models? List at least two, and explain why this is the case.

10b. Write down the names of three people who have either studied the same subject as you or share similar interests and have built a successful career out of their subject or interest (or despite it). Use the internet for research if you cannot think of examples.

10c. If you were to get a career mentor in the next three to six months, what would you do to track and engage your mentor?

NOTES

CHAPTER 11

Building your network

· ·

THE TENETS

11.1 Some say it's who you know, not what you know; I say your legwork and network determine your net worth.

11.2 In stressful environments where systems are shallow and innovation fallow, you have two options: you either work hard or you work hard.

11.3 You might organically build a network of friends and emotional buddies, but you must consciously and strategically build a network of career-enhancers.

11.4 When you stop thinking of university as a place for students and start thinking of it as a space for budding young professionals, your perception and capacity for networking grows.

· ·

It almost sounds pretentious to emphasise the importance of building your network. I have heard many people talk about the importance of who you know, not what you know. I would paraphrase this as 'it is not your legwork but your network that determines your net worth'. (Sorry, I know I am rhyming again!) As convincing as that sounds, though, it devalues the importance of hard work and perseverance and jeopardises the essence of the Graduate Code. So really it should read 'your legwork and network determine your net worth'. That sounds much better.

I have said in many graduate career speeches that in my opinion there are two paths to career success: either you work hard, or you work hard. (I'm afraid there's no getting around this fact!) This is particularly true in a stressful environment like Africa where systems are shallow and innovations fallow. And while I am a true advocate of working hard, in today's pressured post-graduation environment, you also need to work smart. Someone recently pointed out that you cannot work smart unless you have already worked hard. Maybe the distinction between working hard and working smart is irrelevant here, but the common thread is that at least you are still working.

A university is the single largest gathering of future (fellow undergraduates) and current (university staff) professionals who are likely to influence your life in some way before, during and after graduation. In other words, your network is already all around you – you just need to work on building it. That quiet student who speaks less but articulates clearly when they do; that loud student who is always in your face but struggles academically, or even that smart cookie who struggles in social situations. These people are potential business partners, employers and employees, and it is worth making the effort to see them as such. (This can be difficult, so use your eagle eye!)

Even though a university provides access to a large network base, it has the potential to restrict you to networking within its own walls. So you need to strategically increase your network outside your university as well. If you already have connections outside university while you are still studying, you are better prepared for the professional world.

(I should tell you here that my undergraduate days were totally devoid of networking. I wasn't even thinking about life after school, so I didn't consider building a good career network. I had friends, don't get me wrong, but that was all they were, friends and acquaintances. My postgraduate studies, however, were a totally different ball game. I was ready, I was precise, and I was aligned.)

While organically building emotional support and friendship networks, be decisive and strategically build a network of career-enhancing people too. Bear in mind that great friends are not necessarily great career enhancers. You may find your career network grows organically without prompting, but in my experience, you need to make a calculated attempt at developing it.

Notice I didn't say *develop your contacts*. This is because you can have good contacts without having a good network, although you do need good contacts to develop a great network. Networking is about making valuable connections and understanding how to navigate and use these connections to increase your value and the value of others in your network. It's about aligning that lead with what you need.

Your capacity to be a good networker is linked to your personality, but it doesn't totally depend on this. In some sense, extroverts seem to have it easier because they are confident to go up to people and get their phone numbers. These people may be able to collect mobile numbers and emails faster than a bank, but is networking really just about collecting and compiling numbers and emails? I have the mobile numbers of a few very powerful and potentially career-enhancing people, but I have never actually been able to speak with them because they don't answer their calls or respond to emails. So what is the point of simply having that phone number or email? Introverts may find it difficult to approach people in the same way and collect their emails and mobile numbers, but this doesn't necessarily put them at a disadvantage.

To elaborate on this, networking is not about collecting numbers and emails but about understanding what you have in common with those whose numbers or emails you collect and using this to develop a two-way relationship.

Let me ask you a quick question here: how many Facebook or Instagram friends do you have? I have asked this question in several professional forums and most professionals have more than 400 people on their contact lists. For students and young graduates, the average figure rises to 1,000 people, based on the different groups they have been part of over the years. Try this simple exercise now. Go online and check the number of Facebook and/or Instagram friends you have. You will probably be surprised at the figure. However, the reality of the situation becomes clear with my next question: How many of these contacts do you have regular conversations with? Less than 200, I bet. (If you have regular conversations with more than 200 contacts out of the 1,000 you have at the moment, you must be a social media obsessive. That is very rare.)

Now to the question that really matters: How many of these contacts know what you do (or what you want to do) in your career? Now this is when the number of social media contacts can become irrelevant. Due to the nature of social media platforms, you tend to use them only to stay connected with friends and acquaintances on a social level. But what about using them to develop your career as well? (Some obviously do this already, but if you currently don't, don't you think you might be missing out on something?) As I mentioned in Chapter 10, I started posting little write-ups on LinkedIn and Instagram of my travels around Africa some two years ago, without trying to make a big thing of it. Guess what? It soon became a big deal, with a large following of people who now are inspired by the challenges and opportunities of working in Africa. Now LinkedIn is a fundamental part of my career development, and the blog has grown so much that it is the premise for another book I am working on, about business in Africa.

You might want to browse through your social media platforms and figure out which friends on your list are social or emotional friends and which are career-enhancing friends. I have a long list of different people on my social media accounts, but guess what? I have spent time working out which categories these people belong in. To do this, I have instigated conversations around what they do or wish to do, and also explained what my career involves. Maybe this is something you should try doing for starters. If you are strategic, areas of mutuality will begin to emerge based on common interests.

Whenever I received a friend request on one of my social media accounts, I used to add people by default, but that soon changed. Now I spend time finding out what they do and how it relates to me. This is a good exercise to characterise my connections – who is a social connection and who is a career connection? (Maybe a third category could be 'who is a social career interest?' Maybe you can make 'mixing business with pleasure' work for you.)

Let me tell you about my networking activities, and hopefully you can draw some lessons from these. It is important to point out here that I didn't learn any of these activities from a book or a manual of any sort. My experience is based on many years of working and travelling all over Africa but also on working with a range of professionals in academia, industry, government and even civil society.

Generally (and this is what works for me), the steps I take to establish a new strategic contact within my network depend on a range of scenarios, and these dictate my style of engagement. Let me see if I can show what I mean.

If the scenario is that I am attending a business forum, seminar or workshop and those attending will be professionals of some sort who I do not yet know, then I take a five-step approach to establishing that all-important contact within my network. This can be summarised as follows:

- Step 1: introduction
- Step 2: investigation
- Step 3: articulation
- Step 4: characterisation
- Step 5: action

First of all, I *introduce* myself by making sure they know what I do. This is where you need to know exactly how to capture what you do in a few words. Here it is important to differentiate yourself to make people interested in finding out more. (You may find it helpful here to refer back to Activity 1, where you described yourself in a hundred words.) When I am doing this, I study their reaction to figure out if there is any sense of them wanting to know more, and then move on to Step 2, *investigation*.

This second step is about trying to get a sense of what the other person does in their work. As they tell me, I try to get a sense of what seems interesting and potentially relevant to my career portfolio. If what they do is relevant or interesting, then I move on to Step 3, *articulation*. This is when I try to establish the relationship between what they do and what I do (or would like to do) by telling them a lot more about what I do. If there is some common ground, it sparks a conversation. Step 3 establishes whether there is enough mutual interest in a potential relationship for me to proceed. (When your time is limited and you are trying to establish a business relationship, the biggest mistake is to waste time establishing a relationship that is headed nowhere.)

If I clearly establish a mutual interest in a potential relationship, then I move onto Step 4, *characterisation*. This is where I try to figure out if what they do is likely to have a positive short-term impact on me or if the relationship will be valuable much further down the line. I also try to work out if they are the key person to progress the relationship with or if they could introduce me to someone else that they know.

Finally, I move on to Step 5, *action*. The particular action I take is dependent on how I have been able to characterise the person. It is important to note that all these steps flow together seamlessly during our dialogue, but I make a mental note of them as the conversation progresses. Sometimes it takes a few minutes to move from one step to the next, and sometimes it takes a lot longer. Sometimes Step 3 (articulation) and Step 4 (characterisation) happen after our conversation is over. This is where I do enough further research on the person and their organisation so I can decide whether to take action.

All this shows that introduction is the first step to establishing great contacts within your network. The other steps are more research-based and strategy-oriented, both of which can be done later on. (This is the reason I argued earlier that an extrovert is not necessarily the best networker, even if they are best at collecting lots of business cards. But I digress.) If, for instance, I establish that I need the contact in the short term, I tend to ask them what they are currently working on, or what they plan to work on in the near future. This forms the basis for an engagement when I do contact them. It is easier for someone to respond positively to you when you offer them some kind of support with their current work while making a request. If I think they will be needed in the longer term, I make a casual contact – I send them an email or text to say it was nice speaking with them and that I look forward to working together at some point when the need arises.

It's tempting to tell a new contact a lot about yourself during a conversation to establish a business contact, but it's better to learn more about them, as this will be your basis for contacting them later. Make sure what you tell them about yourself is sufficient and strategic enough for them to remember you when you contact them later. As a personal rule, I always end the conversation by agreeing a simple follow-up action. This could be something like 'I'll drop you an email', 'I'll send you a text', 'I'll call you sometime next week', or even 'I'll send you a proposal' if the conversation was good enough to warrant that. Of course, it is important to follow through with any agreed action. There are people who gather lots of business cards at meetings but never use them, and that makes the difference between gathering contacts and building a network.

If you are going to a forum and you know the names of those attending, you could start Steps 2, 3 and 4 in advance by checking out the people you are interested in beforehand. This means that when you meet them, you have a lot more control because you are well informed. You can use the engagement process to confirm what you already know, and this accelerates engagements. Trust me, no matter who the person is, they are always intrigued when you already know their background, and they are more interested in getting to know you too.

Some contacts are totally unplanned, for example when you meet the person at an event or while flying to a meeting. Others are orchestrated to achieve a specific objective. But whatever the case, building your network is about first understanding *what* you want, and secondly about *who* you think can help you achieve that. This way you are always ready to network. Networking is all about understanding who the person is, what they want and why they want this. Only then can you develop the right strategy to give them what *they* want while getting what *you* want. Building your network takes time, and while it may happen organically, it should also be developed strategically.

It gets better and easier to network over time and with consistent practice. I have friends who call me a consummate networker, and I wouldn't have it any other way. My work involves arranging collaborations, developing strategic partnerships, arranging business deals and resolving partnership issues, and being a great networker is one of my top priorities. So I thought I would give you some insights into the personal habits I have developed over time to meet my needs and the overwhelming demand from clients to be a navigator and 'Mr Fix-it'.

The result of my networking activities is that I now have over 2,000 professional members of my network from different industry sectors and at different career levels, from about 48 African countries. (Guess how I save these contacts in my phone? I will tell you shortly.)

At some point in my career development I knew I wanted to be a strategist and expert on Africa. It was also obvious that I couldn't do this without knowing Africa properly, and I couldn't be an expert on Africa without any contacts there. At that stage, I only had Nigerian contacts in my phone, as I was born and grew up there, and some in the UK, where I had studied. Africa is made up of 54 countries, so there was a long way to go. And so I got to work.

Did you realise that there are so many students and staff from different cultures, social backgrounds and walks of life within your university? In the UK, the situation is even more interesting, as universities pride themselves on the number of international students they have from different countries. Lancaster University has students from over a hundred countries, and this is the norm in truly international universities. (It is not necessarily the case that most African universities have students from other countries. I cannot see how a university can be truly international if it doesn't capture an international dimension in its student and staff portfolio, but that is a topic for another book.)

My point is, my desire to be a strategist on Africa was strengthened because the first network base I developed was with international students at Lancaster University from different African countries. Each time I met an African student, I wanted to know which country they were from, what they did and what they intended to do after their studies. Many of my current networks in African countries began with student connections I made during my PhD studies in Lancaster. If you also want to be an expert on Africa, you might struggle to begin building your network with other African students unless your university is truly international.

Once you have a clear idea of your career direction – which I hope by this time you do – then you need to capitalise on the diversity in the student community around you.

Let me ask you a rhetorical question here. Do you know what work your friends' or classmates' parents do? Don't you think it's important to ask or find out? You may well share a class with the children of potential employers and not be aware of this. Or perhaps you have spent the last four years in the same class as potential business sponsors or partners without realising. If you stop thinking of university as a place for students and start thinking of it as a space for young professionals, you start to crack the Graduate Code.

For international students, there is an even more interesting factor which should make you engage differently with the students you meet. When you consider tuition fees, accommodation costs and the price of eating and travelling, studying overseas is very expensive. Doesn't this mean that the average international student you meet is potentially from a family or is affiliated with an organisation that can afford such exorbitant fees? Don't you think you are missing a trick by not getting to know students a little more strategically to enhance your future career objectives? I understand that might sound a little self-centred, but this is reality; everything captured in this book is about self-awareness, appreciation and enhancement of your skills if you do not want to be relegated to the unemployment shelf.

Going back to building my network, the next thing I did a lot was to respond more to Facebook requests from professionals in other African countries. I searched carefully on LinkedIn for professionals from other African countries with similar career interests to mine, introduced myself and what I did and then went through the five network-building steps with them. Whenever I went to an event – whether it was a workshop, seminar or conference – I did something that my colleagues found strange. When other people were trying to get the business cards and mobile numbers of the guest speakers, I was interested in finding out who was in the room who had links, connections or institutional affiliations in an African country I hadn't yet developed enough contacts in. On many occasions I went as far as approaching the registration desk and looking at the names or affiliations registered to try and figure out who in the room had an African connection. They became the people I was interested in, and before long they became part of my network. I have written to and visited several high commissions (embassies) of different African countries and used that as a basis for increasing my knowledge of and contacts in those countries.

At face value, you might not consider a country's high commission as being a significant place to visit. You may even think they are only there to help you get a visa. But when I realised that they were the closest I would ever get to some African countries of interest, their high commissions went from being just physical locations to professional network institutions.

By the way, I didn't forget the question I asked earlier. Do you want to know how I save contacts in my phone? I will tell you. I start with the country, then the name of the person, then their affiliation. Something like this: 'Mozambique Dr Akanimo Odon Envirofly'. You may be wondering why I do this, and my answer is that it alludes to the importance of developing organisational affiliations as part of your career progression. We'll deal with this in Chapter 12. First, though, let's use Activity 11 to help you begin building a great career network.

ACTIVITY 11

11a. How many friends do you have on social media? Of this number, how many do you have interesting and regular conversations with?

11b. Take your time to look at the contacts on your current social media platforms. List the 50 who have the most potential to have a positive impact on your career.

11c. Take your time browsing different career platforms. List ten people who are not currently on your contact list but have the potential to have a positive impact on your career.

11d. In the next three to six months, what will you do to engage the contacts in 11b and 11c in a way which relates to your career (or future career)?

11e. In the next three to six months, try to practise Steps 1 to 5 of the networking process with at least five new contacts, and record your challenges and/or successes.

NOTES

CHAPTER 12

Improving your affiliations

· ·

THE TENETS

12.1   Whether you're a student, graduate or professional, understanding the importance of affiliations drives a conscious effort to seek collaborations that bring career fruition.

12.2   While you develop network contacts with relevant individuals, make sure you learn about and develop affiliations with their organisations too.

12.3   You are only as good as the company you keep. Likewise, you are only as proficient as the professional bodies you are associated with.

· ·

At several graduate and career sessions I have held, I have asked the question, 'How many affiliations do you have?' I rarely see students or graduates with more than two affiliations. Generally, their core affiliation is the university they are studying at and the second is the company or organisation where they had their student internship or work placement. Working professionals may be affiliated with their workplace, former university and a few professional bodies they are members of, but the last of these are often just there to make their CV look good.

Do these affiliations help with career growth? Maybe. Let me give you a sense of what I mean.

During my first degree, just like most students I had two affiliations: the university and the student society I was president of, the National Association of Zoology Students (NAZS). Later on, I added two more: the organisation where I did my student internship – the Nigerian Institute of Oceanography and Marine Research (NIOMR) in Lagos – and Platinum Bank, where I did my national youth service. During that five-year period, I only had four organisational affiliations. I was naive and thought these were enough. At the end of my three years as a PhD student, however, I had over 25 affiliations. So what had changed? I had started to think more about my career and had realised I needed to make a conscious effort to seek affiliations. But what kind of affiliations do you need, and why are they important?

The idea of the Graduate Code is to show you how to start the process of professionalism (or get a taste of it) before you actually become a professional. A significant part of the book so far has dealt with developing yourself and your skills, knowledge and links with other professionals, be they mentors or contacts. This session moves away from looking at your network of people and deals with developing institutional and organisational affiliations.

It is important to develop organisational affiliations that are not just people-based. If you are only affiliated with a particular institution because of a single contact you have there, if they leave the company you lose any affiliation with that organisation, however beneficial your relationship with that particular person might be in other ways.

There are many types of affiliation that you can start to develop as part of your career development plans. These include professional bodies, academic societies, professional groups, network organisations and private and public enterprises. A good starting point is to develop your organisational affiliations alongside your personal contacts and/or network. For example, I got to know a professor of environmental ecotoxicology when he was my tutor; he then became a mentor and later still became an important network contact, and through him I established significant affiliations with several important organisations in Nigeria – the University of Benin, the Nigerian Environmental Society, Igbinedion University and the Centre for Global Eco-Innovation – all of which he is involved with. So while you are developing a contact with an individual, make sure you learn a lot about their organisations too. Then, using your contact person as leverage, try and get to know at least one other person within that organisation. This increases your affiliation beyond a single individual.

A good way to look at which organisations your career best relates to is if you classify them into four organisational tiers, each relating to different aspects of professional life.

- Academia: teaching and research
- Government: policy and governance
- Industry: value and profit
- Civil societies/NGOs: causes and rights

Your overall intention is to build affiliations with organisations whose mandate fits with your career direction. A mandate is the core objective and basis for the establishment of that organisation, and is the key driver of their activities, programmes and expenditure. This provides an opportunity for you to engage with them. The idea of an organisational affiliation provides you with the basis for enhancing your employment, enterprise and educational opportunities, something we already looked at in Chapter 4.

We have already seen that one of the biggest crises with graduate careers is the fact that academia, industry, government and NGOs are disconnected from each other. So when a student or young professional develops an affiliation with more than one of these organisational tiers, they are always better placed than the average graduate. Not only are they exposed to the opportunities these organisations offer, but you also understand holistically how they are related, which can help you develop your career. Let me explain further by using examples of my affiliations within consultancy, one of my career directions. (Note that I developed all these affiliations while I was still a student, but at that stage I had figured out what I wanted to do in my future consultancy career.) Looking at the four organisational tiers above, here are some of the affiliations I have developed:

- Academia: Various universities in Nigeria, including the University of Benin, University of Uyo and Benson Idahosa University
- Government: Lagos State Ministry of the Environment, the National Universities Commission, the Federal Institute of Industrial Research, Oshodi, and the Nigerian Institute of Oceanography and Marine Research (among others)
- Industry: Stopford Projects and BG Group
- Civil societies/NGOs: the British Council, the Nigerian Environmental Society and the Xn Foundation

I have attended conferences and seminars and have been involved with projects and career-enhancing opportunities with all these organisations because they are affiliations. Over time, some of these affiliations have developed into organisations becoming strategic partners, clients and even sponsors within my career portfolio. However, this wasn't the case at the beginning. It began with me wanting to be affiliated with them on different fronts, mostly through participating in their workshops, attending their seminars, taking their courses, joining their groups and networks and keeping them on my radar even when I was a student and not directly involved with many of them.

Affiliation starts with learning about relevant organisations and following what they do. In an era where every organisation has a website and most are on social media, following them is easy and practical. Spend your time developing these affiliations. It was because I had the British Council on my radar that I knew about their annual International Student Awards (Shine Awards) in the UK, was able to enter myself and won Best International Student in 2006. Winning the award changed my life and jump-started the educational management aspect of my consulting career.

Before I completed my PhD, I was aware of many employment opportunities within my affiliations which I could readily apply for, and because I was affiliated with them on different levels, I knew what they did and what the different job roles involved. Let me tell you what else I knew about these affiliations. I knew the scholarship opportunities they offered, the sponsored courses they were running, the annual seminars and conferences they held, how much they had spent in their last financial year and what they had spent it on, the programmes and projects they were planning to roll out the following year, the partnerships they had signed and why they had signed them, any media issues they had had and how they had dealt with them, the partnerships they still needed and why they needed them, and so on. Imagine for a minute if you knew all this information about your key affiliations and organisations and could use it to develop your career. Let me capture what this means in a short analysis.

By the end of the second year of my PhD course, I had attended more than ten workshop seminars, won two national student awards and three international fellowships, participated at student level in three organisational projects and programmes and delivered two student consultancy opportunities, all because I was affiliated and involved with organisations relevant to my career. And the most interesting thing about all this? It cost me virtually nothing to take part in these. My only costs were my time and creativity, which included learning how to write compelling letters requesting sponsorships, networking to figure out who to approach to attend a workshop for free or who to contact to get involved in a project. Most of these didn't involve travel, but they formed the bedrock of what I do now. Fast forward twelve years, and I believe I have now mastered using affiliations to enhance my career objectives. In 2016 and 2017 alone, I travelled to over 20 African countries, delivering seminars, granting interviews, participating in conferences, advising governments, arranging partnerships, supporting young people and so on. But guess what is even more interesting? Of these countries I visited, the only time I paid for my international travel, accommodation and food was a trip to Nigeria for a family holiday. My affiliations covered the costs of all the other trips.

An important affiliation, mostly talked about within the context of a graduate career, is memberships of professional bodies. It is considered important enough to be a subsection of a traditional CV, most often named 'Professional Bodies and Affiliations'. While most people focus on professional bodies as their main career affiliations, this chapter has shown that affiliations should be a lot wider and more encompassing than that. However, the role of recognised and reputable professional bodies as part of your career development profile is very important.

I attended a career workshop on one occasion during my studies where the facilitator mentioned that professional bodies are meant to be the most informed organisation around their relevant subject. They are supposed to have the most up-to-date and globally relevant information and guidance that pertains to a professional group. One thing they are pretty good at is keeping their members up to date with this sort of information, which they do by producing and sending out newsletters, brochures and briefs, developing and delivering professional training courses, organising and hosting events and promoting a wide range of information and opportunities about and for their members.

During my undergraduate studies, I was totally clueless about what professional bodies were and the important role they played. From conversations with other professionals, most have confessed that they only saw the point of developing affiliations with professional bodies after they had become professionals. Imagine if they had been affiliated with these organisations before they were professionals. Since most of these local and international professional bodies offer student memberships, you can almost certainly become a member. There are different levels of membership – student, graduate, affiliate, associate, full and chartered, the latter of which most aspire to. Some offer fellowships, which are the highest level awarded by a professional body. Your membership level is mostly achieved by your professional expertise, duration of membership and contributions, and is sometimes proven by taking a written examination.

In most African countries, the professional body around accounting and finance is the most prominent and highly regarded, and this is because of the reputation of chartered accountants. There is nothing to stop you from being a member of several professional bodies, so don't limit yourself. You can even become a member of a professional body without having core expertise in the subject matter you are interested in. This is what the affiliate membership level is usually designed for.

Are you still wondering what was on my ten-page CV? Well, when towards the end of my studies I realised the importance of being affiliated with a professional body, I went all out. I became a member of seven professional bodies, some directly related to the subject I studied and some which were relevant and interesting to me. This gave me plenty of material to write about.

In summary, being affiliated with professional bodies will involve the following: joining these professional bodies (both locally and overseas), preparing for and taking professional courses (if possible), and attending professional events and programmes.

You must have heard the saying that you are only as good as the company you keep. Well, I dare say you are only as proficient as the professional bodies you are associated with. With that in mind, let's start thinking in Activity 12 about how you might begin a new era of developing your affiliations.

· ·

ACTIVITY 12

12a. List three academic, three industry, three govern-ment and three civil society/NGOs whose mandates relate to your course of study or professional career space.

12b. List five professional bodies (local and international) associated with your course of study or professional career space.

12c. List five activities that you will do to engage better with one or more of these organisational tiers and professional bodies in the next six months.

NOTES

CHAPTER 13

Researching an interest

THE TENETS

13.1 If research is a mandatory requirement for graduation, then it must also be a compulsory component for career progression and sustainable professions.

13.2 Move from knowing what the different types of career routes are to describing why they fit, and how they are the best fit for you.

13.3 In every graduate area are challenges waiting to be resolved; assume a professional's status and see opportunities waiting to be explored.

13.4 The inquisitive graduate mind that asks a lot of questions soon becomes the professional heart that provides a lot of solutions; therein lies the power of research.

The above definition contains two phrases I wish to draw your attention to – 'systematic investigation' and 'establishing facts and reaching new conclusions'. I will come back to these in a minute.

Research is a fundamental component of education and learning. It is so important that globally, all final-year university students must undertake a research project of some sort and/or write a dissertation in order to be awarded a degree. In most international universities in Africa and overseas, the idea of research is fully integrated into the course curriculum, especially in institutions that require students to write reports and essays. These essays require you to do some form of research into a subject before you are able to critically respond to the question(s) set. This is not the case for courses based solely on examinations, but you still must do a research project of some sort. And if it's mandatory, it must be pretty important, don't you think?

It is vital to undertake a research project as part of a master's degree, and a doctorate is entirely based around research. Okay, education is only one of the three career routes that I identified in Chapter 4, 'Choosing your career route(s)', but let's now think about the other two core routes to a graduate career – enterprise and employment. When you realise that enterprise is based on providing a service or supplying a product to meet a need or demand, I think you already know the answer. Just for starters, you have to figure out what the market needs, why it needs it, how you can meet that need, when you should meet that need, what to charge to meet that need, who else is trying to meet the same need and how they are meeting that need currently. And the list goes on. Every question you ask forms the bedrock of a successful enterprise. Remember the above definition of research? You have to systematically investigate in order to reach new conclusions, and there's no getting away from research if you want to be successful.

It is little wonder that the bigger an enterprise gets – and I am talking about huge multinational companies here – the greater its focus on research. These companies almost always have a research and development (R & D for short) department. Small and medium-sized companies may not always have a full department dedicated to research, but trust me when I tell you it is the only way they can survive. Research is even more crucial as they have less money to spend and have to learn to improvise.

And what about the employment route? Well, unless you are working for an alien on Mars, the work environment is driven by research. Not only do you work for an enterprise which needs research to survive, but you are constantly required to be attentive and creative. Even when your work is mundane and routine, what separates you from the others is you knowing a lot more than they do. Though minimal, you cannot overemphasise the significance of doing your research. The Graduate Code cannot be complete without a discussion of the topic.

I'll tell you something I have noticed, though. Students, graduates and young professionals are usually not great at research. Or maybe they just don't enjoy it?

I remember doing the research for my undergraduate disser-tation and it was an absolute nightmare. I really struggled. I was in a university system – as I imagine most of you still are – where independence was an alien concept. We had to depend on the lecturer for everything. They came into class, read the lecture notes to us, answered one or two questions and left the room again. And in some cases, they didn't even turn up. They just sent the lecture notes to the class representative and he read them to us. I only attended classes because I had to, rather than because I enjoyed them. Anyway, my course was completely based on writ-ten examinations. I have no idea how I got a first-class degree. (To be fair, I think I know how I did: I 'ate up' the lecture notes and regurgitated them back to the examiner exactly as I had been given them. Simple. It was called 'cramming'. It still is. A friend made a joke that you upload the content of the lecture notes to your biological hard drive a few days before the examinations, walk really carefully into the examination hall so the information doesn't spill out, download the notes to the papers and at last you are free. Try asking many students one month after examinations what they studied in their programmes, and if they remember the content, they are better than I ever was. I asked this in a forum once and a student answered, 'Try one week, doc.' So one month afterwards was pushing it if just a week was enough for them to forget everything they had learnt.)

Imagine my misfortunes, then, when I began my master's degree in the UK. The lecturer used to come into class one day a week to teach, and midway he asked the class what they thought. As simple and straightforward as that question seemed, it shook me to the core. I wondered why he was asking what we thought. No lecturer had ever asked me that question. It didn't make sense to me. 'Don't ask me what *I* think, tell me what *you* think, Mr Lecturer, and that will be good enough for me,' I thought. (Don't blame me, friends, it was the higher education system I was groomed in. I had been totally dependent on my lecturers in Nigeria. Little wonder that I was clueless about researching and finding things out for myself. I will return to the danger of overdependence on your university teachers in Chapter 20.)

In the UK, and in a few African universities I have been involved with, intellectual independence is the norm and the lecturer acts as a guide. This is indicated by the fact that the systems were not only examination-based – we also had to produce lots of independent essays, reports and coursework. All this independent work in the UK exposed me for the first time to the fundamentals of research and writing. My examination questions changed from things like 'What are the different types of career routes that exist? Please describe them' to 'There are three types of career direction. Describe how you might choose the route that is best for you.' This system put power in my hands. It gave me my space and brought to life the power of analysis and expression. I am a business consultant, but I work in policy, law, media, management, agriculture and science, among other things. There is a reason I am able to navigate these different subjects, and it has to do with my capacity for research and my ability to crystallise and articulate information in a manner that shows my views and perspectives. If you follow me on social media, you will notice I write short posts that cover a wide range of areas, but they get better with practice.

Look around you, and what do you see?

As I travel throughout Africa, I see a lot of things. I see a child in dire need of food. I see young graduates desperately looking for work. I see a human resource manager looking for someone amazing to fill that new position. I see a guest speaker trying to communicate his thoughts to an audience. I see, I see, and I see lots of challenges.

As a consultant, I see a lot of challenges too. I see a young man trying to get the funds together to start a consulting firm. I see a young lady trying to figure out how to write a business plan for her new venture. I see a consultant wanting to understand how to raise funds to grow their business. I see a Tanzanian university wanting to establish a strategic partnership with a UK institution but not knowing how to go about it.

In my creative media career, I definitely see a lot of challenges. I see young movie scriptwriters who do not know how to translate their scripts to film. I see young producers looking for the next round of funding to start or complete their productions. I see a content creator looking for the best platforms to promote and market their content. I see a company director seeking the best agency to develop a television commercial for its new product. I see, I see, and I see lots of challenges.

Every challenge you see is the basis for an opportunity. It creates an opportunity to provide a solution to that challenge. But first you need to find out a little bit more about the challenge.

Most of the challenges I listed whether within my consulting or creative media career portfolios (which, by the way, are pretty random) actually do have some answers and solutions which already exist. However, you still need to find out which solutions already exist and how these can be adapted to resolve the challenge, and this still boils down to researching your interest. Most people immediately turn to Google if a question comes up which they don't have an answer to (you hear the expression 'google it' all the time). How about taking some time to google your areas of interest and help you understand what is happening in your field of study or professional work in other jurisdictions, industry sectors or scenarios?

If you think you now know all there is to know about your area(s) of expertise or professional interests, you are living on Fantasy Island. There is always something new: new information, a new process, a new consumer, a new competitor, a new application, a new research paper, a new policy that you could learn about. Some of these might not be new to others but still new to you. Getting in the habit of researching your interests always places you a step above your peers.

Always begin any research with a question. Everyone who has done research, whether quantitative or qualitative, knows that worthwhile research always starts with a question. What exactly are you trying to figure out? Why do you want to figure it out? How will you figure it out? Who will benefit if you figure it out? Where might you figure it out? These questions engage your curious side, and if you craft them well, you can systematically carry out an investigation to discover the answers.

If you want to succeed in your career, you must always ask questions. The university system is supposed to encourage the level of independence required to spark creativity and ingenuity. So if like me you are (or were) being guided in a system where you depended on your professors, you need to step back and learn how to find things out for yourself.

In Chapter 11, I mentioned that I decided to become a strategist and expert on Africa, but what use is an African expert who doesn't know enough about Africa? So seven years ago, I decided that every other day I would learn some new information or data about the continent. Oh, I have learnt a lot and I have so much data at my fingertips to fuel what I do and how I respond to situations, but guess what? I still have an unbelievable amount to learn. Learning never stops.

It might surprise you to learn that I don't generally enjoy reading. I read for examinations and for work, because I have to, but when it comes to reading for pleasure and knowledge, I used to struggle. However, when I discovered that I tend to retain more information when I read for pleasure, I realised that this makes me stand out. After making this discovery, I started reading a lot more about topics that interest me. Someone walked up to me at the end of a gender summit in Rwanda several months ago and said, 'Doc, your session was the most interesting, and you know why?' Obviously, being a curious person, I asked her why, and she said, 'Every time you had to respond to a question or make a statement, you backed it up with a trend, data or extra information which emphasised the point a lot more than explaining it.' And she was correct.

Do you know what the topic of my undergraduate degree research dissertation was? It was on the impact of oil spills on non-target species. Do you know what the topic of my master's degree research thesis was? It was the impact of soil amendments on plant growth. And for my doctorate degree, my thesis was on the impact of pesticides on non-target species. What do you notice that flows through nine years of study in higher education institutions? I seem to have a thing for impact. It's a fascination with cause and effect, action and reaction. (Thinking about impact, what might the impact of reading this book be on your career progression?)

It was the research project during my undergraduate degree course (albeit immaturely and probably uncoordinatedly) that fuelled my sense of wanting to delve into the realms of environmental management as a career direction. It was the first time I had fully believed that even though I was studying zoology, I could see a career in protecting the environment from oil spills. I believed it because I knew I would do it. When you do what you believe, it eradicates disbelief and brings relief. It definitely did for me.

We have established employment and employability as fundamental crises facing the African continent, and these are issues that can be resolved on different fronts. However, I already know about a model that helps to bridge the unemployability gap, something I learnt about in the UK. In the Lancaster Environment Centre at Lancaster University, the largest university department, there are 24 resident small- and medium-sized enterprises (SMEs) on the premises. Once a year, the university emails these companies, asking them to develop a short research project which could, they believe, provide solutions to any of their business problems if properly carried out and written up. These could be one-month, two-month or even six-month research projects. An example in law might be 'What are the legal frameworks that could support the growth of my business in China?' In business, it might be 'Who are the best customers of my new business product and service?' In engineering, it might be 'Why is this engineering process being used in Ghana and not in Cameroon?' It is all about asking questions. (And just in case you were wondering how I know all this, my consulting firm is one of those 24 SMEs. You didn't see that coming, did you?)

All these SMEs, including mine, write up these questions as research projects and hand them over to the university's central business management department. This department then advertises these research projects to undergraduate and postgraduate students, who have to bid and apply for these projects to become their dissertations or theses. So basically, you have a student who is doing a research project for a company down the road who needs the results of the research to improve their operations, or you have a student doing a dissertation that a company is waiting to use to start a new product line. How genius is that? Simply fantastic. Now this is the kind of research that the Graduate Code promotes. These students are already student consultants, carrying out a piece of work that is in demand and provides a solution to a challenge that someone is actually facing. This is power. This is starting a professional career even before you leave the walls of a university. This is what the Graduate Code is about – preparing you to live a great graduate career.

So when you start to plan your next research project, you might want to consider two things – choosing a topic that actually interests you, and making sure it is a response to an actual challenge and provides a solution, no matter how small. And if you want to start becoming a professional, I suggest you put a reminder in your diary to carry out a piece of independent research every three months or so that brings to light something new about your interest and career direction. You won't regret it.

To get you thinking through the issues discussed in this chapter, here are some activities for you to crack on with. Note that for Activity 13c, I am trying to get you to research career opportunities outside your country of birth or residence. To respond to this activity, you will first need to choose three countries, learn about their national policies and programmes and find out what happens in those countries in relation to your planned career and areas of interest before you can assess the challenges and opportunities. I will deal more with overseas opportunities in Part III of this book.

ACTIVITY 13

13a. Write down three research questions that aim to investigate something new and interesting about your course subject, hobby or career direction.

13b. List three challenges that students on your course face regularly. (If you are already a professional, list three challenges that professionals within your field of expertise face regularly.)

13c. Write a two- to three-page piece on the topic 'What are the national policies, programmes, and career challenges and opportunities in your area of interest in three countries, not including your country of birth or residence?'

NOTES

NOTES

CHAPTER 14

Starting something new

. . . .

THE TENETS

14.1   People say ideas rule the world, but if thinkers rule their ideas, then making ideas happen is what actually rules the world.

14.2   There are student, graduate and professional ideas. Some are bad, some are good and others are great, but how can you tell which are which? Critique them. Test them. Apply them.

14.3   Never underestimate the power of universities or their affiliations to provide a great environment to test and grow ideas without all the animosities and challenges that come with such actions in the outside world.

. . . .

A common saying is that ideas rule the world. While I appreciate this saying to some extent, is it true? If ideas rule the world, what rules ideas? In my mind, the owner of the idea does. You may have all the ideas in the world, but what use are these if they remain concepts inside your head? I would rather you said 'Making ideas happen is what rules the world.' You get my drift?

It is somewhat easy to come up with ideas. By this I mean both good and bad ones, but still ideas. Everyone has ideas about something, but it doesn't make them good ideas. There are bad ideas, there are good ideas and there are great ideas, but how can you say which are bad, good or great? Critique them. Test them. Apply them.

I have come across many young graduates and professionals who have told me about really amazing ideas of what they would like to do to enhance their careers. I have received hundreds and hundreds of emails and DMs on my social media platforms from people who wish to make a difference, many of whom have amazing ideas. And while some are amazing ideas today, many won't be amazing ideas tomorrow. But how will you know whether your ideas could be useful today if you don't test them?

I discovered rather late in my career that a university provides a great environment to test and grow ideas without all the animosities and challenges associated with similar actions in the outside world. Why is a university a good place to test and develop ideas? There are a few reasons I can think of.

The first is that you have access to facilities at little or no cost. I don't know about you, but each time I go into a university, I see a lot of facilities that can be used to test an idea – access to venues for events, access to libraries for research, access to the internet to gather and research information, laboratories for testing chemical reactions, and so on. (You're probably thinking here that I must be referring to UK universities or expensive private universities in Africa. I appreciate that these facilities are not available in all universities, but if there is a need, there is always a way. Stick with me for a minute.)

Secondly, you have access to experts, by whom I mean the large number of professors in universities. Do you realise that many of these are also consultants to multinational companies and the government? (I can hear you saying 'But how can I share my ideas with my professor? He would wonder why I am doing something else and not focusing on his lecture notes.' You may be right, but if you don't try, you will never know.)

Thirdly, you have access to the student community and staff, ideal customers and audiences for your ideas. How many students are registered at your university? Are they potential customers to test your ideas on or with? Are they potential partners in helping you realise your grand idea? Are they potential clients? Will they benefit from your new plan? They are all of this, and much more. (Again you might wonder how you can reach these students. The answer is that they are all around you, and all you need to do is ask.) I do not even need to say 'where there is a will, there is a way', because for this there is already an express way. To be honest, I don't say that phrase in a blind-faith kind of way, even though I am a strong believer in the power of faith. It is said with conviction and understanding that you are left in a bubble of impossibility just because you have not done anything to search the Google of possibility.

The reason why I have worked with universities up until now and why my consulting office is within one is that I have tested their benefits first-hand and they are without a doubt good places to come up with and develop ideas. (Don't worry, I won't be giving you examples of some of the ideas I had back in the day!)

But before we get to this benefit of universities, let's go back to the importance of trying to develop your ideas within the confines of a university environment. When you are a student, besides the fact that the university can provide a lot of resources at little or no cost, you don't usually have the pressure of caring for anyone else. It is also a good time to develop a few interests and see how they play out.

If you have already done the activities in Chapters 1–13, I would imagine that by now you will have a sense of your main interests and career direction, even if it's just a sense at this stage. The idea of this chapter is to get you to start doing something about these, no matter how small. And remember, there is something else you have a lot of as a student. Time.

Now let me paint you a picture, this time focusing on professionals.

I meet professionals all the time, and there are no people as full of ideas as working professionals. However early on they are in their careers, they have seen things they never saw or considered while at university. They have been exposed to the market space and what people want. If they have specialised in an area of interest, they have enough of a sense of the challenges within that profession to come up with ideas of what to do about them. And for those working in areas that are not necessarily part of their desired career and do not support their interests but which bring in enough money to keep body and soul together, they also have clearer ideas of what they would like to do. Like I said earlier, ideas are never lacking.

How come so many professionals have lots of ideas but find it difficult to get them off the ground? Do you know the answer? They probably have money to jump-start the idea but no time. And if they do have the time, it is difficult to develop an idea on a trial basis if they have the pressure of family depending on them. I will look at family pressures in Chapter 16, but the point is that at this stage many professionals wish they could be back at university, testing that idea and building it so it is ready to 'plug and play' after graduation. (Well, this this is exactly how I felt – and still feel, I must say – so I assume I'm not the only one.)

Never before have I had ideas like the ones I have now. It's like a stream flowing endlessly, but I don't have the luxury of testing everything I believe would work. One thing, though, that most professionals fail to do is consider their university at this stage as a good location to take the pressure off when testing an idea. For some reason, it never crosses their mind. As far as they are concerned, they are graduates and have moved on. I am not so sure that is true. There is a word that still binds you to your university, even if you are now a working professional, and it is the word 'alumnus'. Yes, that university remains your alma mater, whether you like it or not.

Do you know where I first tested my idea of writing the Graduate Code as a book? At the University of Benin in Nigeria and Lancaster University in the UK – my alma maters. Do you know where I first tested if my consultancy company would function okay? At those same universities. Do you know where I first tested my idea of establishing a charity organisation in the UK, a charity which later I co-founded? At Lancaster University. I will tell you a bit more about these shortly, but I want to make it clear that being a working professional doesn't limit your access to facilities, professionals, experts, personnel, customers, clients, partners and the like within the confines of a university (or at least its affiliations).

I can hear someone saying that I have no idea how difficult these universities can be. Really? Is that based on your opinion, or on an actual connection? If you are a young professional, at least, you have been working for less than ten years, and that is not too long ago to start a conversation with your alma mater.

Let me make something clear here. I suggest approaching your alma mater because it is probably easier to re-establish a conversation with them for a progressive discussion on building a strategic partnership. But the university in question doesn't necessarily have to be your alma mater. The chances are that if you are a working professional, you are within driving distance of a university. You should get used to thinking of a university as a strategic partner for life, because that is exactly what they are. Whether you are in employment, enterprise or you plan to go into further education, a university is significant to you on some level. So you might as well start getting friendly with a few.

When I suggest starting something small, I mean starting something easy but important, and it's even better if it is something new that is a primer or precursor to your career direction. The previous chapter focused on researching an interest. This is just a starting point. What information have you discovered – or what idea have you had – which you think and believe can solve a particular problem? Now you might have a grand idea, but the emphasis here is for you to start something small. When you start small, you have control. Exploring your theory differentiates and separates you from most of your peers as a 'doer' and not just an 'ideas person'. It then gives you the confidence to translate an idea into an action (no matter how small), and with this new-found confidence you can aim higher and bigger. The aspect that seems to scare many people is the fear of failure. At least you are starting small, and so it is easier to cope with failure. Most importantly, you can learn enough from the experience to make failure less likely the next time.

Every project, business or solution to a problem begins with an action as part of the implementation process. As they say, 'The journey of a thousand miles starts with a single step'. What will your first step be? There is a big difference between having an idea or thinking of something new you wish to do, and actually doing something about it.

So what can you do first, and what can you do now?

Starting something small can begin in a number of ways.

Firstly, if the idea makes sense to you, tell someone you trust about it and make an effort to develop it.

Secondly, write it down so that it can be shared with interested parties or sponsors, especially if you don't have the resources to make it happen.

Thirdly, break it down into different phases of implementation, taking into consideration what you have and what you need. Ultimately, don't think too much about it; just do it.

Let me illustrate from personal experience how an idea can grow.

I was in my office working on my PhD one day when I received an email from a senior government employee in Nigeria. They wanted to visit the UK and asked if I could arrange the trip and for them to meet with a strategic partner for discussions on a collaborative working relationship. I sorted out the arrangements and sourced the person they needed to meet, and the trip was organised on that basis. In return, I was offered minimal remuneration for arranging something which was totally unexpected.

This gave me the idea that people might be interested in visiting the UK from African countries. I was a student so couldn't do much about it, but I realised that I could start something small. I made contacts with a good friend, Professor Samuel Guobadia of Igbinedion University, Nigeria, and we agreed to collaboratively organise a one-day conference at Lancaster University that I called Academia for Green Africa (AFGA).

To get this event started, I developed a proposal and pitched it to my department as an event to strengthen strategic partnerships between Lancaster University and African institutions on environmental matters. As an environmental department with a growing interest in Africa, they loved the idea and agreed to sponsor it. They provided the venue, the meals, the facilities and sent invitations to Nigerian participants who were interested in visiting the UK and developing strategic partnerships with Lancaster University. Guess who the main guest speakers at Lancaster University were for the AFGA event? Yes, my two PhD supervisors – Professor Kevin Jones and Professor Kirk Semple. Some high-level dignitaries flew in from Nigeria and it was a successful event. It began as just an idea, but I started small and managed to organise an event I didn't need to spend a penny putting together. Never underestimate the power of starting something small and using the support of your university.

Guess what happened after the AFGA event? It became clear to me that there was a consultancy niche in helping establish strategic partnerships between UK and African organisations, and this is now a core component of my consulting firm. It started with a first step, a first action which was successful and provided an opportunity to develop the idea further after my studies. Since then – and fast forward ten years – I have hosted in excess of 1,000 African guests in the UK at different events, seminars, conferences and business forums.

In the process of starting something small and new, don't underestimate the importance of allies. A good team is fundamental, especially when you are trying to start something new and exciting and have no resources. What you have is a great student community, or, if you are a professional, a group of professional friends. If you can get these allies to buy into your idea, you can get a lot of benefit from their contribution and make it happen. This was the premise and basis of another project I started as a student over 12 years ago. Let me share it with you quickly.

In March 2007, it occurred to me that there was no umbrella event that brought Nigerian students together, and with an average of about 20,000 Nigerian students studying in the UK annually, it felt like a truly great event to put together. I felt good about the idea, although it would remain just an idea unless I did something about it. So I spoke to two friends and got them to buy in to the idea. We named the event the International Conference of Nigerian Students (ICONS), and we got to work. As with the AFGA conference, we pitched the event to the international office of Lancaster University and they bought into the idea and agreed to sponsor it. We then advertised the event and hosted about 180 Nigerian students from all over the UK at Lancaster University for two days. It was the birth of something truly remarkable, but it began with an action and a first step.

It was not an easy ride – we had to organise this huge event while in the middle of our postgraduate studies – but it was a collective vision that made sense. Fast forward to now, and ICONS has become the single largest programme for Nigerian students in the UK. In the past eleven years, this programme has been hosted by seven UK universities, sponsored by over 60 institutions, including university and business sponsors, involved over 20,000 Nigerian students, provided an opportunity for the delivery of over 50 workshop seminars to over 5,000 students, and has garnered over 150 top guest speakers including high commissioners, ministers, chief executives, members of parliament and a host of other dignitaries. The most recent event, in 2018, transitioned from being the International Conference of Nigerian Students (ICONS) to become the International Student Conference for Africa (TISCA), expanding to cover students in the UK from other African countries.

With your mind on some of the ideas you have and how you could jump-start them with minimal or no resources, let's move on to Activity 14.

. . . .

ACTIVITY 14

14a. Come up with three ideas that you think you can start to implement without needing any funds.

14b. What resources would you need to start any one of the ideas listed in Activity 14a? Where and how would you get these resources at no cost?

14c. If you were given 10,000 USD today, what would you choose to buy to grow one of the ideas listed in Activity 14a?

NOTES

NOTES

CHAPTER 15

Furthering your education

. . . .

THE TENETS

15.1 In a highly competitive environment where most who are looking for professional or executive work have an undergraduate degree, furthering your education is a great differentiator with a competitive advantage.

15.2 Whatever your route to choosing a programme, enjoy it the second time round and ensure it expands your career opportunities and progression.

15.3 To avoid pitfalls in furthering your education, consider the five clear factors of engagement: the Programme, the Place, the Provision, the Pathway and the Plan.

. . . .

Why is this an important chapter, you wonder? Well, it is based on personal experience. One of the biggest worries that an undergraduate (and even a working professional!) faces is how they can remain relevant among the competition. You might remember how I decided to do my master's degree in the UK. I simply walked into the library at my dad's office and went through the huge Association of Commonwealth Universities (ACU) guide book. If you did that today, you would be stuck in the past.

Generally, when you complete your undergraduate studies, there is a small voice in your head telling you that it would be nice to do a master's degree. Some folks complete their first degree and get a job right away, which is amazing. But for some reason, five years down the line many want to resign from their jobs and undertake a master's degree programme. Others enjoy their jobs too much or perhaps can't give up their salaries because of family and dependents, and sign up for master's degrees by distance learning just to keep work and study going. Others still resort to master's degrees just because they have been sat at home jobless after completing their undergraduate degree programme. And when you are stuck at home, with your parents choosing every opportunity to slip in a comment about your joblessness, you want to get out, don't you?

The truth is that everyone loves to be a master of their craft, and why shouldn't they? A large percentage of people complete their undergraduate studies and can't get a job and see doing a master's degree as the alternative, but is this the right approach?

Now I know that I spoke in Chapter 4 about the three E-routes – Employment, Enterprise and (further) Education – and even though you choose just one of these routes immediately after your undergraduate studies, you might well need all of them at different times in your career. In a highly competitive environment where most people looking for professional or executive work have an undergraduate degree, having a second degree (in this case a master's degree) is a great differentiator and gives you a powerful competitive advantage.

But don't misunderstand me. It doesn't make sense to go through an undergraduate programme you don't like and then progress onto a further education programme that you don't like either. It is important to enjoy what you choose for your master's degree, but make sure it provides you with a clear path for career progression and success. It makes all the more sense for you to consider and plan for further education as early as possible, rather than it being thrust upon you as an alternative, during which major mistakes tend to happen. One thing is clear, though: at least during your master's degree you have a second chance to maximise your career potential using the tenets of the Graduate Code laid out clearly in this book. (I hope you have been taking part in the activities, because these will help you lay a clear path to developing your career.)

To avoid unnecessary pitfalls in furthering your studies, I have given the points to consider five labels: programme, place, provisions, pathways and the plan. If I may, I would like to call this the 5 key points of consideration (KPC) for Education Progression. I think it has a nice ring to it.

Okay, let's start with the *programme* you want to study.

In line with furthering your education, which could be wanting to do a master's degree or doctorate, choosing your study programme should be the first point of consideration. (It doesn't actually have to be either a master's degree or a PhD. It can just as easily be a diploma or a certificated programme of some sort.) Considering how many students tell me they haven't enjoyed their first degree, it's probably a good idea to get your next programme right, don't you think?

There are three ways to decide your programme. You could choose to specialise in an area you enjoyed in your previous programme (for me, this was doing a master's degree in environmental management, a subject which had been a module in my zoology degree), such as a master's in supply chain management, a module in many business management degrees. Or you could choose a new area to study that you have worked in, even if it appears unconnected with your first degree programme, such as a friend who did a master's in business development after working in a bank for five years, even though his first degree had been in chemistry. Or you could embark on a course programme which you have neither studied or worked in but which complies with current demands and aligns with societal relevance, like a good friend of mine who read engineering at university and then went on to do a master's in professional accounting.

Whatever your route to choosing a programme, what is most important is that you are happy doing it and that it expands your opportunities and career progression after you have finished studying. There are some questions you do need to ask yourself, though. Why do you think you should further your education? Is it to be much better placed than your contemporaries in a competitive job market? Is it to gain the knowledge and skills required to be better at your current job? Is it to put yourself in a better position to be promoted? Is it to increase your profile and proficiency, especially in your consulting role or a new company you have set up? Whatever the reason driving further study, the programme you choose must be relevant in the workplace or at least complement or augment your capacity for enterprise.

It is also important to think about the name of the programme, and it is worth comparing similarly named programmes and investigating what the modules within each programme cover to know if your course is unique. You need to also consider the model of delivery – full-time, part-time or via distance learning – and this will depend on the time and resources you have available. Finally, consider a programme that allows you to learn and take modules from other disciplines as part of the course, even if they are optional. It is important to understand the programme requirements from the very start so that you can work towards them.

Generally, postgraduate programmes are either taught or research in nature. While taught programmes generally include a series of taught modules, requirements for you to write some essays and reports and take an examination, you ultimately have to carry out a short research project. Research programmes fundamentally involve what their name suggests – research. These involve mandatory work with your research supervisor to determine your research objectives, plans and procedures, and like a taught master's, your examination involves writing a long report, which could be a dissertation or a thesis. People who immediately go onto a research degree such as a PhD after taking a taught master's degree tend to stay in academia, but not always. Some have other reasons for doing a PhD. Most people who go back to work after their taught degree and later come back to do a research degree do it for the profile and added proficiency it gives. I am an exception to the rule, like most others in similar positions to me. I went onto a research degree immediately after a taught master's, but by the second year of my PhD I knew I wasn't going to remain in research. At least I figured out what I was going to do with my research degree before I concluded it. Many don't.

It is important therefore that you know what programme you wish to undertake and why. A mentor has a great role to play at this stage of your life (refer to Chapter 10 if you need a reminder).

Another important consideration is the role that distance learning and short courses can play in furthering your education. Not everyone is able to do a one- or two-year master's degree full-time, but furthering your education is paramount in increasing the expertise, skills and knowledge you need to enhance your proficiency and/or profile in different career sectors.

Distance learning gives many people the flexibility to make up for the time restrictions they have. In the same vein, certified short courses provide a good basis for furthering your education at a lower cost than doing a full-time degree-awarding programme. (I am not saying that short courses should necessarily replace degree programmes, but at least they are a justifiable alternative.) Some distance-learning degree programmes now take into account the fact that flexibility is crucial for most learners who need this model of education delivery. As such, these programmes have now introduced three levels of exit within a single course. You can now take a collection of modules within a structured degree programme, and if you cannot continue you can exit but still be awarded a degree. The main exit degrees are a Postgraduate Certificate, a Postgraduate Diploma and then, upon concluding your research project, you get a master's degree. As some of these programmes charge you tuition fees per module (and in some cases per exit route), you can plan better and grow your expertise with reasonable convenience.

The term Massive Open Online Courses (MOOCs) has recently been unleashed onto the education market. MOOCs are yet another way to further your education with some elements of flexibility and choice. They are strategic short online courses, mostly designed in an introductory format to give you the fundamentals of a subject matter, with primers to help you work out what longer courses you could do if you so wish. They are free and developed by a wide range of international institutions, and you would normally be required to spend between two and seven hours weekly to complete an average MOOC. Just imagine taking a collection of MOOCs over a relatively short period of time and getting certificates for this learning. Oh yes, most of them are now certified, though you might pay a small fee for the certificates.

Once you are clear which programme you wish to undertake, the next thing is deciding where you wish to study that programme – the *place*. Generally, you decide the place you wish to study alongside considering the financial demands of the course and the resources you have – the *provisions*. Which country do you wish to study in, your home country or overseas? If you want to study in your home country, which university has the best programme for you? If overseas, which country/countries would you consider going to?

Let's deal with studying overseas first, and then we can look at studying in your home country.

Popular overseas study destinations include the United Kingdom, USA, Canada and Australia. These are great and reputable overseas destinations, but they can be expensive. When I say expensive, I mean considering tuition fees, travel costs and living expenses. Costs can range from around 25,000 USD to 50,000 USD per year all-inclusive depending on the programme of choice, location and ranking of the institution, with the high-ranking universities costing much more. There are lower-cost study destinations for Africans which include Malaysia, China, India and Singapore in Asia, and Germany, Ukraine, Hungary and the Netherlands in Europe.

Internationally, universities are ranked in their regions using different indices. The common ones include teaching quality, research quality, student satisfaction, employability after graduation, web presence and international outlook. As I like to tell those who ask, consider a university's ranking, but don't kill yourself to get into a high-ranking institution, especially if your financial resources are low. If you can, strive for truly high-ranking universities – but remember that most ranking data are subjective and user-defined. (For example, if I want to do a research degree, and a university has a highly reputable international research portfolio, do I care if it has the worst web presence?) Make sure that the university is truly international and that studying there would have a positive impact on your profile and proficiency.

You will need to spend some time browsing the internet to find out a lot of this information – or better still, seek the help of a registered and approved education recruitment agent. There are several of these agents in different countries, but make sure they are registered by the approved body in that region. Studying overseas is great for exposure, strategic partnerships and increased knowledge of global models, but it mostly comes down to being able to afford it. Little wonder it is one of the biggest challenges many people face. In such circumstances, three key things come into consideration: scholarships, fees payable by instalment and working while studying. Other considerations include loans, sponsorships and bursaries.

One of the most common questions when it comes to overseas studies is around scholarships. Who offers scholarships? How do you find them? How do you apply for them?

Generally, scholarships vary in value, as there are part and full scholarships. There are national scholarships given by countries and states, and there are scholarships given by particular agencies such as the Commonwealth, British Council and United Nations. There are scholarships offered by particular universities, and there are scholarships offered by corporate organisations. If you want to obtain a scholarship to further your studies, you need to put in the work. You need to search out and apply for as many as possible. You need to know in advance when they are likely to be advertised, based on when and how they have been advertised in previous years. You need to spend time browsing the internet and checking out scholarship platforms and offers.

You do have to understand something, though: international education is fast becoming a revenue generator for institutions and states, and so there are always fewer scholarships than there are people wanting them. This means that you need to be strategic and precise in your preparation for sourcing scholarships. Firstly, think about the course you wish to do, and then start getting all the necessary documentation together in preparation for applying for scholarships. Sometimes you can apply for a scholarship and course at the same time, but most scholarship applications require you to have been offered a place on a course first. This usually means you need to submit an admission offer letter as part of your scholarship application. It is important to get everything in place to apply for admission early, so you are not under pressure to get an admission offer letter when the deadline for a scholarship application is upon you.

So what kind of documents do you need? Based on my experience of institutions all over the world, you will need the following to apply for admission for a longer degree:

- an admission application form (of course!)
- your results (a transcript or statement of result or degree certificate)
- references (from a work and or academic referee)
- your CV (I am glad we covered this in Chapter 7!)
- a personal statement of purpose (a high-level statement showing why you wish to study that course, what you intend to get out of it and what you wish to do when you graduate)
- a research proposal (if you are applying for a research-based master's degree or a PhD)

Some international institutions also require you to submit evidence of proficiency in the language of the programme, which can be passing a language examination (such as the IELTS, the International English Language Testing System) or showing that your previous degree was undertaken in that specific language. Other institutions may waive this element if you have previously scored above a particular grade in that language.

As well as scholarships, you might consider supporting your further studies financially by working while studying. Most overseas countries have legal restrictions on the amount of paid work you can do while studying, and it is important to comply with these restrictions. So unless you are undertaking a part-time programme, you cannot expect to cover all your financial needs from working. At present, however, most overseas destinations restrict the number of study visas available for individuals wanting to study part-time, and that places you in a fix. You would normally only be granted a visa for a full-time study programme, and this limits the number of hours you can work.

Now, maybe it is also worth considering destinations that don't require you to have a visa to resume your studies, have limited restrictions on working while studying, or even allow you to study part-time while working. A note of warning, though. It is vital to create a balance between working and studying, because it is difficult (if not impossible) to study full-time while working full-time and still achieve great academic results. Obviously it boils down to the individual, but it is something to keep in mind. If you are studying full-time, especially for a higher degree, it is important to focus and get the best out of it.

In some cases, you may be more likely to find someone to sponsor you if you can pay your tuition fees in instalments. This means you would need to consider institutions that allow you to do this. Most overseas institutions allow you to do this, provided you agree to their terms and conditions, which dictate how often payments should be made and how much you should pay each time.

Generally, further study in your home country is less expensive than going overseas, and you do not have to worry about visa issues or work restrictions. Ultimately, though, it is crucial to seek advice from experts to help you make the right choices – and trust me, there is help out there – but you can at least make a start by browsing the internet and finding out things yourself.

The last few paragraphs covered important considerations that should guide your choice of *programme* and *place* based on the *provisions* available to you. With these in play, the next thing is to investigate and understand the career *pathways* provided by the programme you wish to undertake, and then *plan* for them. In some cases, the advertisement for the programme itself gives a sense of possible career pathways, but in most cases you need to find these out yourself. The career pathways for your programme of choice are the potential that is available to you, but you need to put things in motion to optimise that opportunity.

Firstly, you need to gain admission to the course.

Start by finding out early what the general admission requirements are, and prepare for them long before the application period. Do the same for scholarship opportunities. (I must admit that none of this crossed my mind during my first degree.) I wonder how many of you thought about it while you were doing your undergraduate degree? You might have considered further education, but did you actually look into it? If not, a simple requirement like getting an academic reference as a mandatory document to obtain admission might not be so simple after all. This is particularly true after you have graduated, especially if you have moved to a different city. It is even more difficult if you were not on great terms with your lecturers while in school and then need to contact them for a reference letter. So it's best to get to know a potential referee while you are still in school, or you might lose a scholarship offer in future.

In terms of your career *pathways* and *plans*, I cannot end this chapter without referring you to an important point. Although this book has been written with young students in mind, it has also been written for young graduates and working professionals. Furthering your studies therefore gives you a great opportunity to apply the tenets of the Graduate Code to your next degree programme. It gives you a second chance to get things right if they went wrong during your previous degree.

It is probably best, then, that we look at Activity 15 and get you to start thinking about the best ways you could further your education.

ACTIVITY 15

15a. List five master's degree programmes you could go into using your first degree programme certificate.

15b. List five postgraduate programmes you could do relating to your hobbies or interests. These should not be related to your first degree course.

15c. List two home and two overseas universities which offer more than three of the programmes listed in Activity 15a and 15b.

15d. Search for and list all the possible scholarships available to you for furthering your studies.

CHAPTER 16

Anticipating and preparing for social pressures

. . . .

THE TENETS

16.1   In graduate careers, skills and capacity are great and vision and planning are fantastic, but never remain in absolute naivety of life's peculiarities and uncertainties.

16.2   Irrespective of external factors and social pressures, it's always best to have clarity and plan for crises before difficulties arise, because in the midst of chaos, logic pales into obscurity.

. . . .

I spent a little time in Chapter 6 talking about the pressure on you to be successful after graduation so you can earn enough to take care of your extended family. This situation is not ideal, but is what most African families expect of their children. However, I have not yet spoken about a more immediate social pressure that could affect your graduate career –starting your own family (for those who wish to go down this route, obviously).

On a personal level, I struggled to write about this aspect of the Graduate Code because it connected with me on an emotional level, and I needed this to be a practical book based on my experiences. But the more I thought about it, the more I felt I would not do justice to reality unless I made things clear. (In some respects, my sense of family won't let this go, so here we are.)

The pressure of having my own family, and the impact it would have on my career, was not something I ever considered while I was studying for my first degree. In fact, it was not something I ever thought about after I graduated and then started my national youth service programme. I knew I wanted my own family one day, but how that choice might affect my career direction was never part of my thought processes. Not even once.

I understand it is impossible to predict when you might fall in love, get married or start a family. (Some people perhaps know precisely when these things will happen. If this is you, I suggest you begin a career as a fortune teller, because it's a good niche. I am sure many people would pay you to tell them their future.) But what if you *did* know? Wouldn't you plan for it? Although many people are sure they will start a family someday, they don't bother planning for this because they don't know when this will happen.

Speaking from experience, I have worked with and trained a lot of people, and I have seen the enormous impact family has on careers. Its significance cannot be overemphasised.

You finish your studies and graduate, then perhaps you get a job in an area you're not necessarily interested in, but it gives you some resources to pay the bills. While you're working there, you meet someone, get married and have a lovely daughter, and now it's no longer just about you. Now you have other people to consider when making strategic decisions. Perhaps you need to further your education by doing a master's degree, but you really can't afford to leave your current job. If you do leave your job, you almost certainly have to consider doing something flexible and enterprising to earn some money while you study.

Maybe a distance-learning course makes sense. Then you won't have to quit your current job at all. But wait a minute. Is it better to finish your studies, including your master's degree – and for the very academic ones, a PhD too – before starting a family? What if you fall in love, get married and then get an offer to do a fully funded PhD overseas, but the funding is only enough to cover your own living costs? What happens if you cannot afford to travel with your spouse as well? I could go on.

The truth is that for every scenario painted above, I personally know someone who had to make that decision. In most of these cases, the person suddenly found themselves in the position of having to make a decision which would have a huge impact on their family, and everything came to a standstill because they had never really considered what to do before then.

That reminds me. Don't forget that your extended family are already expecting you to provide for them, so you need to consider them alongside the needs of your immediate family. As you cannot get around this, you need to think (within the boundaries of reason!) about what you might do if one of the above situations was to arise.

When you have your own family, you end up interacting differently with people (and with different types of people) and making different decisions about possible career scenarios. As I am writing this I cannot help but think that the situation is generally a little more complicated for women than it is for men. So here I am going to go down the gender route, because this is the reality most people face. Besides, I consider myself a strong advocate of gender parity and equity, and do not wish to forget the importance of female empowerment as a fundamental topic on the career growth agenda. Because *The Graduate Code* is based on African experiences, however, I particularly want to emphasise the impact gender has on career progression. The impact of gender in Africa is significant to say the least, more so than in most other places, and it is something that I believe young women should consider when they plan their careers within the tenets of the Graduate Code. So let me start by painting you a picture if I may. Stay with me, ladies, because this is serious stuff. And gentlemen, you need to know this because it will change your perception. Well, I hope it does, anyway.

The university environment is balanced in terms of gender equality, at least better than most other environments: men and women have access to the same education, services, opportunities to better themselves and the same foundation for a successful graduate career. How come this changes after graduation? Let's take South Africa as an example. According to the *University World News*, in 2018 58% of students in South African universities were women, while 42% were men. There were more women than men at lecturer (53%) and junior lecturer (57%) level in South Africa, but at senior lecturer levels, the percentage of women dropped to 45%. Do you notice a trend? Oh yes – the numbers drop as people progress in their careers. By the time we get to the highest-level role in a university, the role of vice chancellor, only 5 of the 26 VCs in the country are women. The situation is the same at school level: 72% of state-paid teachers are women, but only 37% of school principals are female. And this is the case in most African institutions, and similar in most industry sectors.

Gender bias in career and work is a big thing, and the earlier you appreciate it the better. The UNDP (United Nations Development Programme) estimates that Africa loses USD 95 billion annually as a result of gender inequality. And according to the African Development Bank, women make up over 50% of the agricultural labour force in Africa but contribute up to 80% of the continent's food even though they receive less than 1% of the credit due (and the sector contributes over 25% of global carbon emissions, so you cannot even tackle climate change without resolving gender issues). Now don't get me started on sustainability, because I won't stop, but I hope I have made my point here.

Getting married and having children are humbling experiences, and working when you have children is particularly difficult in an environment like Africa where there are fewer gender-specific support systems (such as paid maternity or paternity leave, flexible working hours or childcare provided as part of the work package). In many cases women lose their jobs when they get pregnant, and some have even been given ultimatums and told they cannot get pregnant if they want to keep their job. How awful is that?

It makes life much easier if you have some level of clarity before you meet your partner, so that you can discuss your career aspirations early on in your relationship. You don't want a partner who will object to and even frustrate your career growth. If you fall in love with someone who knows and respects you, including all you are and want to be, it makes things much easier, and there will be fewer obstacles to your career in future. I know I am being idealistic – and I also appreciate that life is not always that straightforward. My point is more that it is always best to have clarity before difficulties arise, because irrespective of external factors, logic can be forgotten in the midst of chaos.

Data shows that there are more male CEOs across different industries and in different economies (more so in developing than developed countries, but the trend is the same). Many more women with graduate degrees fail to progress in academic careers than men, more women drop off the career ladder than men, and the list goes on.

Before you accuse me here of supporting only women, men also get caught in this social career net that makes it difficult for them to do what they want. Many men are caught in a career trap, keeping quiet about work problems and facing all the nonsense and frustration a job they hate throws at them just so they can provide for their family. After all, aren't they the 'head of the household'? When this is the case, the idea of changing careers can seem like a non-existent option if it jeopardises their economic security.

The key point of this chapter, to which I will now return, is that having a good plan, or some sort of plan, is always better than having none. (This is the point where I could say 'to fail to plan is to plan to fail', but this is not always the case. Sometimes you just don't know what to plan for when the cards are still in the pack.)

For me, especially in relation to careers and the impact of social, family or gender-based pressures, planning involves thinking about potential alternatives in case things don't go according to plan. It's about you planning for the unplanned, even if you're lucky enough to never need your fallback plan.

Let me paint you a picture here.

Have you noticed that many women who graduate and can't get a job (or get a job but are unable to grow in their professional role due to their family situation) end up either starting a small business of their own around their children or starting a flexible course that they can fit around family life? Does this tell you anything? Well, think again back to Chapter 4, 'Choosing your career route(s)', where I talked about the three E-routes post-graduation – Employment, Enterprise, Education (and perhaps the fourth, Entitlement). Considering these routes helps you to plan in advance for them, but it also means that if for any reason social pressures affect your capacity for employment, at least you have the option of enterprise to fall back on. Many people choose to start small businesses when they are under pressure and they have no other option. Many of these businesses are set up when chaos seems to abound. Now imagine if you had plenty of time to think about what kind of business you could start *before* the need for it arose. Don't you think you might be more organised?

In 2017, I founded and launched the Young African Women Initiative (YAWI), an enterprise development, strategic leadership and sustainable business programme for young women in middle and senior management. I held the first programme, a five-day course, in Lusaka, Zambia. As I delivered training to over 25 top female executives from the extractive (mining) sector, it was a delight to see their passion and enthusiasm to make a difference. As I listened to the issues and challenges they faced in the corporate world, I couldn't help but think that things really need to change in Africa. Female empowerment in Africa should not pay lip service to an agenda – practical action needs to be taken, with the premise that if we don't get it right, Africa won't make it.

Let me get philosophical for a minute, if I may. What is empowerment or capacity-building within an African context? Is it providing knowledge and resources that change lives, or is it giving people the right support to change their own lives? Is it giving people jobs and income, or is it providing the right environment for people to create jobs and income for themselves and for others? Or is it a combination of both?

As I delivered a mentoring session with these incredible young female executives in Lusaka, it soon became clear that one of the biggest challenges they were facing as women was complete disrespect or cynical enthusiasm about their competencies, especially from their male counterparts. I cannot tell you how much that saddened me. But then I was re-energised when they started talking about their visions and aspirations for national development. They seemed to have unconsciously figured out a way to include sustainability in their plans, something which I suspect is tied to their maternal disposition. (One woman even said to me, 'I manage my home effectively and yet they don't believe I can manage projects.' I wonder who 'they' are.) My point is that while it is great to have skills and capacity to deliver, and fantastic to have plans and visions, it is naive to think that these alone will get you through life. If you make plans while remaining aware of life's peculiarities and uncertainties, you will be able to get through most difficulties if you stay confident and focused.

There is always some kind of pressure, and you will encounter social pressure in the future, so prepare for it now if you can – and if you are already in that position, navigate it appropriately. But how? you might ask. I hope to deal with this in Part III, but first let's use Activity 16 to look at how you might deal with social pressures now you have a clearer picture of the situation facing you.

. . . .

ACTIVITY 16

16a. List three social pressures you are facing or have faced as a student or young professional.

16b. Explain how that affected or is affecting your career growth and development.

16c. Write down what you think you should do now, or what you would have done differently at the time, to help you cope with these social pressures.

NOTES

NOTES

PART III

Enhancing the Graduate Code

....

This part looks at societal and international factors, information to support your graduate career experiences, and the next steps you need to take.

CHAPTER 17

Realising your light-bulb moment

· ·

THE TENETS

17.1 If you don't know what you're supposed to be doing in your career, you still can work it out, but if you do know, then you should do it. Seek your light-bulb moment!

17.2 Align your personality with your professionalism, because then your graduate career will be fun, not hectic.

17.3 There is a difference between that light-bulb moment of realisation and daylight period of actualisation. Take vital steps to make your realisation a reality.

· ·

Most successful people will tell you that there was a particular moment in their career when everything suddenly made sense. This tends to be called the light-bulb moment. For many people, it was a moment of awesome, almost explosive clarity, and for others it wasn't so dramatic. And to be honest, it doesn't *need* to be dramatic. You don't need to suddenly have career clarity while caught in a multi-billion-dollar-enthused trance.

I wish I'd gone into a trance and heard a voice telling me what I was supposed to be doing. Even though that didn't happen to me, though, there was a specific point in my life when I suddenly knew that I was supposed to be a navigator and connector. At that time, it didn't click that it would require me to become a proper Ajala, a real traveller. That came much later. But I do remember my light-bulb moment.

In the first year of my doctorate degree I was not on full funding, and so I was working two jobs while trying to keep my hours well within the number allowed for international students under UK immigration law, at that time 20 hours per week. I worked as a cleaner at the indoor market and as a pot washer in an Italian restaurant, both in Lancaster city centre. A few days a week, to make up my hours, I also began work as a carer in a home for the elderly in Morecambe, a large town a few miles from Lancaster. It was not easy mixing it with doing my PhD, but I needed to pay the bills.

It was in March 2006 that everything changed for me.

Out of over 2,000 international students who applied, I had just been named Best International Student in the United Kingdom at the British Council's prestigious Shine Awards. I was invited to a reception at 10 Downing Street with then British Prime Minister Tony Blair, and this was followed by a series of other receptions, including one at the Nigeria High Commission in London and another with the then Nigerian Minister of Youth and Sport, Frank Nweke Jr. After that I was asked to go to Nigeria for a few media engagements, which included interviews in national newspapers, television programmes and even an event hosted by the British Council in Nigeria where I had to give a short motivational talk to young people who were invited.

During all of these events I had to engage with different people, and I was also looking forward to talking about my PhD programme and the research I was undertaking. I remember clearly that for some reason, most of the people I tried talking to about my PhD were not particularly interested in the topic. What they were interested in was how I could help them with sponsorships overseas, how I could connect their institutions with my institution in the UK, how

I could help them get funding for their research work, how I could organise a training programme for them in the UK and if I knew of a technical partner in the UK for a potential contract they were wanting to apply for. For them, it was all about the connections my new media leverage could bring. Do you see a pattern here?

In the wake of the media frenzy in the UK and back home in Nigeria, and with the platform this coverage gave me, I co-founded an NGO, Xn Foundation, with a friend, Mr Benedict Okhumale. Along with some other friends – Bamidele Adebisi, Ife Akintunde and Justice Akpan – we launched the International Conference of Nigerian Students (ICONS), which aimed to increase creativity and promote positive ideals for Nigerian young people, and to encourage them in the middle of a 'brain drain' crisis to return and contribute to their home country at the end of their courses. (You may remember me talking about this conference in Chapter 14). This conference was to be the first of several – there has been one in the UK every year since, for the last eleven years. The first conference of Nigerian students, which Lancaster University hosted and sponsored together with the British Council in Nigeria, showed me that I could become a connector between Nigerian students in the UK and their careers back home in Nigeria after graduation.

Not long after ICONS took place, I had a request from Nigeria from an individual who wanted a connection in the UK. I made the connection rather easily – through a simple online search – and was surprised when the person in question offered to pay me for my work. As well as being a pleasant job which I had found relatively easy, this event also showed me that I had the potential to get paid for being a connector. This was my light-bulb moment. To be fair, I didn't feel the hairs on my arm stand on end or go into ecstasies. It just suddenly made sense. My light-bulb moment was therefore more like a collection of clues and opportunities that presented themselves as my career progressed, and I decided to explore it extensively.

CASE STUDY 1: WHEN FURTHER STUDIES LEAD YOU TO YOUR LIGHT-BULB MOMENT

I have a good friend who is currently juggling a demanding full-time job heading a policy department in an agricultural development organisation in Tanzania and running a nutrition business and a foundation alongside a career in politics pursuing the transformation of her country's policies. Her name is Neema Lugangira, and she is a formidable and passionate lady. I was speaking with her recently about light-bulb moments, and I was able to pinpoint the moment when it became crystal clear to her what she needed to do to jump-start a new era in her career. For her, this light-bulb moment was during her master's degree, when she was studying in France for an MBA in purchasing and supply chain management. She chose her dissertation specifically to empower her for a new career in local content. This decision was timely and the topic was unique because Tanzania had just discovered huge amounts of gas, and local content was about to become a big deal there.

This top professional didn't simply carve out a nice portfolio for herself – she also triggered a chain reaction of interests when her dissertation was published as a book, one of the first indigenous books on local content in Tanzania. Little wonder that since finishing her studies, she has worked at Statoil, the Ministry of Energy and Minerals, the Prime Minister's Office (under the National Economic Empowerment Council), championed local content policy in Tanzania and has acted as a local content consultant for a long list of organisations. She had her light-bulb moment, and it lit up her career path and has fuelled everything she has done since she completed her postgraduate education in 2013. When I asked Neema what advice she had for students, her response was poignant. She said, 'Whatever it is you do, let your research or thesis shape you, because it is your first official attempt at investigating a societal challenge or developing a solution, but most importantly discovering your niche.' This ties in nicely with what we looked at in Chapter 13, 'Researching an interest', and she couldn't have said it better. (By the way, I didn't mention that Neema is just 36 years old and a mother of two teenage children. Now that, in my opinion, is impressive.)

CASE STUDY 2: BUILDING ON A PASSION AWAKENED DURING A FIRST DEGREE

Talking about having your light-bulb moment when conducting research, it was a little different for another friend of mine, Tato Herbert Nyirenda, a Zambian academic and researcher teaching at Copperbelt University in Kitwe, Zambia. For Tato, his light-bulb moment was not an explosive one. Rather, it was a careful progression into his career niche and a gradual awakening of what he enjoyed doing, and with the right skills and opportunity he moved into and embraced that career space. In Zambia, there were few choices at the time, and even though he wanted to do something in genomics, he ended up doing a first degree in demography, with a minor in economics. Soon he realised he had a passion for health issues, and so did a postgraduate degree in public health, with emphasis on health policy and economics. However, his light-bulb moment framed his career, because even during his first degree he found a love for research and data analysis, and came up with the idea of charging a fee to help fellow students with their research work. Little wonder that he chose to become an academic in the end – his love for research and making an impact has been able to reach its full potential. As he said to me, everyone has big career plans, but ultimately, when you find yourself in a career space that looks impossible to navigate, you need to create a pathway through it with determination and guidance. This is the overall premise of the Graduate Code, and Tato is living it as we speak.

There is a big jump between that light-bulb moment of realisation and the daylight period of actualisation, where you start taking steps to make that light-bulb moment a reality. As the saying goes, make hay while the sun shines – and do it before night time comes, when no man can work. Many people already know what they are

171

supposed to be doing, or what they would like to be doing, but they need to learn how to do this. It is particularly tough for those who are already working in an area that they seem to have built a career in. For these people, who normally rely on this work to pay the bills, they often don't know where to start even though they want to move on. Others don't quite know what it is they are supposed to be doing and need to untangle the idea in their mind.

It is of course possible to have more than one light-bulb moment. Since having my first light-bulb moment, I have had several more, each sparking an idea which complemented my current and future career. I talked earlier about the importance of having a variety of possible career pathways that you can develop. What normally happens is that these career pathways end up prioritising themselves depending on the levels of satisfaction and relaxation they give you, and you find yourself spending more time and resources on one in particular. So in some sense, a student might struggle to work out what they are supposed to be doing, but a professional is more likely to know the answer (in a career sense, at least).

Another very important point to note is that a light-bulb moment may not lead you directly to what you should be doing. Sometimes it can actually be a moment where you realise what you are not supposed to be doing.

This might sound strange at first, but think about it for a minute. If you knew clearly that you were on the wrong path and weren't enjoying what you were doing, would you carry on doing the same thing if you had the option of doing something else? In the second year of my PhD, I realised clearly that I was not cut out to be a laboratory-based researcher, even though my entire doctorate was based on laboratory research. Lab work is routine and requires patience, careful planning and execution, but it requires a lot less strategic insight and innovation – well, mine did. I flourish when I have to be spontaneously creative and push the boundaries of ideas, which is why strategy comes easily to me. A laboratory job would limit my imagination and the freedom I have in my career. Even though I didn't clearly know what I needed to be doing career-wise at this point, I definitely knew what I was not supposed to be doing, and so I totally avoided investing my time and resources in it. My poor but lovely PhD supervisor knew I was struggling, and struggle I did. It's no wonder that during my PhD I wrote and published a book of poetry titled *Rhymes from the Heart* (for your information, the book had nothing to do with pesticides or laboratory processes). It's also unsurprising that this was the period in which I chose to co-found an NGO that focused on increasing creativity and opportunities for young people. I needed an escape route – but I also needed to develop my passion, and this is a crucial point I will pick up in the next chapter.

Talking of developing passions, a colleague of mine, Dr Melba Wasunna from Nairobi, Kenya, a very formidable legal professional who chairs the Strathmore Extractives Industry Centre (SEIC) and Extractives Baraza, says, 'I started off as a corporate lawyer, transitioned to academia and now work for Kenya's biggest mining company. A law degree allows you to be flexible. We are not all meant to be litigators in court, nor are we all talented in that capacity. The skills you learn in law school – especially critical thinking and analysis – are easily transferable.'

So in some sense you need to know where your strengths lie and let your career choice align nicely with them, or else you will struggle.

You might take on a new job that is exciting and invigorating, especially when you first start it. There is the sweet feeling of having a new job, especially if you have been looking for one for a while. There is also the immediate gratification of being valued enough to be paid to provide a service, irrespective of how mundane the job is. But then what happens a year later? Will you still feel great about that job, or will you be seeking to move on? Did you know when you first took that new job that it was just a stepping stone to something greater? Did it occur to you from the beginning that you wouldn't really enjoy the job (perhaps because it didn't align with your passion and personality) but decide to take it anyway just to gain experience? All these reasons for taking a job are fine, but you should at least know why you are doing that job when you are actually doing it. What mostly happens is that you start a job, and before you know it, you have been doing the same thing for five years. When you sit back and look at what you have achieved, you realise that you have spent most of those five years feeling miserable and frustrated. To make the situation even worse, you have been so consumed with the job you most definitely do not enjoy that you have not invested any time or energy in things you do enjoy. So being aware of what you want to do, or at least having a sense of knowing this, is everything. Dr Wasunna puts it very powerfully: 'Don't divorce your personality from your career choices. That way, it won't feel like work, but simply a part of who you are.'

If you do not know what you are supposed to be doing, you still have time to work it out, but if you already know where you need to be, you need to make this happen. The most common thing I hear from different professionals is that they no longer feel fulfilled in their roles and want something more challenging. Many feel like they have wasted their time for too long, while others need something to get them back on track. Whatever point you are at in your career, you can still get things back on track. I think it is important to get a clear perspective to challenge a huge mistake many professionals make, and I hope to deal with this in the next chapter. Do stick around.

In the meantime, let's move on to Activity 17, and think about your light-bulb moment.

ACTIVITY 17

17a.   When would you say your light-bulb moment was?

17b.   What have you done since having your light-bulb moment? (If you have not done anything yet, what do you think you could have done since having that light-bulb moment?)

17c.   Based on your personality, passions and current position, try listing at least five career pathways you think you would struggle with.

NOTES

CHAPTER 18

Making up for lost time

. . . .

THE TENETS

18.1   To make up for lost time in your career, let go of the feelings of desperation and imbibe the feeling of affirmation, because there is always time for transformation, and this time is now.

18.2   To make up for lost time in your career, you need a quantum leap, so invest, invest and invest until you see a change.

. . . .

If you have read up to this point, I imagine you feel one of three things. Let me see if I am right.

Firstly, you might be feeling a sense of vindication. If that is how you feel after reading this far, you must be at the top of your professional game. I am absolutely delighted that you have been affirmed in your belief that the things you have practised and excelled at was worth it, and it brings me pleasure that I have managed to clearly capture the value of this process in the pages of this book. Can I say, though, that this feeling of vindication is not very common. Even though I am writing this book, I am not yet at the top of my professional game and still feel that I have a lot of career to improve on. I am still growing my career and looking to make things better with every step I take and every move I make (excuse the musical reference).

If you do feel a sense of excitement and delight from having aligned yourself to the tenets of the Graduate Code already, I have just one simple proposition. This is that I suggest you should make it a point of duty to inform and influence others who are struggling (if you have not been doing so already). I use the word 'duty' carefully; in my opinion, part of being human means you have an obligation to help others in need. Apologies if that sounds like I am moralising. I am just trying to make a case for sharing the lessons of the Graduate Code for the intended good it might bring.

There is a second feeling, however, that I imagine many will have at this stage, and it is very different from the feeling of vindication. Instead, it is a feeling of regretful dissatisfaction. I suspect this is how most of you feel at this point in the book, and it is a feeling I know only too well – because it is the exact feeling that drove me to write *The Graduate Code* in the first place, that all-consuming feeling of 'I wish I had known these things a long time ago' or 'I wish someone had told me these things when I was still a student' or the classic and simple 'Had I known what I know now...' The most positive thing about that feeling, I have to say, is the subtle – or maybe graphic – realisation that something is not right with the status quo, followed by an appreciation of the fact that you could have done things better if you had known what you now know. Hold that thought for a minute and let me dig a little deeper, because I think this is fundamentally important.

Now if a feeling of regretful dissatisfaction engulfs you, or if it has engulfed you as you turned the pages of this book, that is totally okay. It is actually a great feeling to have at this point in the book, because it means that change could happen. What matters most is how you feel *after* you acknowledge your feelings of regret. Here, I think there are three possible reactions that might follow on from regretful dissatisfaction. The first is indifference. There is not a lot I can do if you cannot be bothered to take any action, so we'll put that to one side. The second possible reaction, I believe, is motivation. This one I absolutely love and advocate for. It is the best place for all my readers to be. If you feel regret but are motivated to make a change, then the Graduate Code has fulfilled its total mission. If you feel this way, I will come back to you shortly. Finally, you may be feeling a sense of resignation. Now this I do not like at all, but I will not totally dismiss this feeling, as it is possible to do a little more work to move you from resignation to motivation. I will also try and explore this a little further in a little while. Before I do that, however, let me put a few things in perspective.

You can work for bills, and you can work for thrills. Most people would prefer to work for thrills. In other words, they want to work and have fun on the job. Once you have figured out what you enjoy and wish to do career-wise, you should strive to invest some time and energy into it. The biggest mistake that many professionals make is that they get too consumed with their current work and do not invest any time or energy into something else alongside that.

Let me ask you a question here. If you invest, say, ten units of energy (this is me being very rhetorical, but hopefully you take my point) in a job you dislike and also invest the same value of energy in a job you like, which do you think would have the furthest quantum leap? I think you know the answer. Now the same would follow if I said that an even smaller amount of energy invested would give a further leap if it was invested in something you were truly passionate about. No matter how stressful or unsatisfying your current career engagements are, it is important to try and invest small amounts of love in that interest you are passionate about.

CASE STUDY 3:
DEVELOPING AN INTEREST INTO A PAID ROLE

This discussion reminds of me of Caludia Togbe, a young professional woman I met recently. Caludia is a diplomat from Benin who has undertaken three master's degrees (which in itself is an impressive feat!). Her postgraduate degrees were in international relations and diplomacy, elections management and international law, and she is currently doing a doctorate in the international law of the seas. Now this is where things get even more interesting. Although she has taken all these degrees, her fundamental interest was always in running her own business, and so she set up a cosmetics company which she now runs alongside trying to complete her doctorate degree. When I asked what her biggest regret was, her response was very simple: 'Not having a clear career plan'. By this she meant that even though the courses she undertook helped her become a confident intellectual and offered some amazing diplomatic opportunities with the African Union and ECOWAS, the Economic Commission of West African States, she wishes she had spent a lot longer developing her profile in business administration. Even though running her cosmetics company started as a hobby, it has become a really powerful and fulfilling dimension of her career. But this only happened because she invested energy into developing it while her main academic activity was as a doctorate degree student. Within two years of starting a new cosmetics brand (Origine Terre), located in Cotonou in the Republic of Benin, as chief executive she has built her company to 12 staff members and increased its product range to more than 60 products. For me this is a great demonstration of a quantum leap when passion is involved. By the way, at just 32 years old Caludia now gets paid to do her hobby, but she has a lot of lost time to make up for, especially after taking her three master's degree courses.

CASE STUDY 4: FINDING YOUR PASSION LATER IN YOUR CAREER

My friend Fredrick Munthali, chief scientist at the National Commission for Science and Technology in Malawi, also had to make up for lost time when he discovered his true passion much later in his career. He had undertaken a first degree in mechanical engineering and then began a private career, spending several years working in production. He then realised his niche lay in the environmental sector and decided to undertake a master's in environmental engineering. As he puts it, this is the best career decision he has ever made, and it laid the foundations for a rapid career route into his niche in research management. He regrets that he spent so long working in an area he didn't really enjoy, but he had the motivation to turn that regret into positivity and now he leads the environmental engineering unit of the nation's regulatory body on science and technology.

In every professional is a student wanting to learn, and in every student is a professional waiting to earn. So if you regret not doing things well when you had an earlier chance but are still motivated to make that change now you know more, it is important to tap into the student in you. You almost have to unlearn a few things while preparing to learn new ones, but the best advice is for you to take some time to complete the activities in this book. This way you can almost retrace your footsteps to work out where you missed opportunities.

For those who feel regret and are starting to sink into resignation, I have some good news for you. After doing a number of assessments with different focus groups while writing this book, it soon became clear that it is much easier for a professional to start the process of change after reading this book than it is for a current student or young graduate. Even though time has passed and you have probably made mistakes, it is pointless crying over spilt milk. You might feel that you have already progressed too far in your career and your professional route seems to be determined. However, if you feel disgust for your job and are completely unmotivated in what you do, you won't last long if you continue like that. You can still make changes (or at least adapt or adopt a few things to make that disgust bearable) and welcome in some feelings of enjoyment to stop your career being a bore. It might make you feel better to realise that you have a list of things at your disposal which a student doesn't. The first is that you have already experienced getting it wrong (or getting it really wrong). This therefore means that you won't get it wrong again. That gives you a huge competitive advantage, if you ask me. The second thing you have going for you is the resources, links, experience and external support systems needed for a change in direction. Most students still have to figure out what these sorts of resources are, as they might not have easy access to these from within the walls of their university. Thirdly, after being a professional for some time, in some sense you already know the things you enjoy or would like to do. In any case, I am sure you know what you definitely dislike, which is how you have reached this point. You need to start by taking little steps towards retracing your footsteps to where you would like to be. This won't be easy, but it is not impossible.

Let's take a look at Activity 18 now, and consider your feelings at this point.

. . . .

ACTIVITY 18

18a. Please write down exactly how you feel at this stage of the book (1. Vindicated; 2. Regretfully dissatisfied, but motivated; 3. Regretfully dissatisfied, but resigned; 4. Another feeling not covered). If you can, explain why you feel this way.

18b. Would you recommend this book to other people? Why or why not?

18c. What do you want to do next?

NOTES

NOTES

CHAPTER 19

Aligning skills for the new era

. . . .

THE TENETS

19.1 It's 'town and gown', not 'gown and town', so always consider the town (society) first and then fashion the gown (academia) to respond to the town's needs and challenges.

19.2 Different skills were relevant during the four industrial revolutions; acquire skills relevant to the current era.

19.3 Irrespective of your field of study or professional space, you should integrate sustainability into that space.

. . . .

I had never used a PowerPoint application before my master's degree studies in the UK. I had to do a main seminar presentation during my first degree in Nigeria, but like most other students I used cardboard posters as that was all I knew. As my master's course had a few presentations embedded in it, I had to develop that skill rather quickly. Likewise, I had never used state-of-the-art data analysis software before I started my PhD, and for a course that had a lot of data to analyse, I had no choice but to learn how to use that kind of software. I was learning skills to stay relevant, and when that relevance was crucial to my success, it gave me an extra push to enhance those skills.

So here is my question: if you knew which skills and knowledge were (or would be) relevant to your current or future national, regional and even global career space, would you try and develop these? (If your answer is no, you might as well stop reading the book at this point and hand it over to someone who would find it more useful.)

You have probably heard the term 'town and gown' used to refer to industry and academia (in another sense, the non-academic population could be seen as the 'town' and the academic community as the 'gown'). For some reason people never really say 'gown and town', and I have always wondered why that is the case. After all, it rhymes whichever way you say it. By implication, though, putting 'town' first is logical. It would make sense for the authorities, government and university management to always consider the town first and then fashion the gown to respond to the needs and challenges of that town. Then we would have functioning and effective institutions that produce graduates whose skills fit with the society or community they are released into. Now wouldn't that be interesting? If we think about it this way, it makes sense to focus on what industries need and use this as a basis for universities to develop and incubate graduates who meet these needs. And if universities are not doing that, then students and graduates must strive to make themselves and their gowns relevant to the town. Here I thought it might be useful to paint you a picture of different industrial revolutions throughout history and show you where we are now, so you can see if you have the skills and knowledge to survive in a new industrial era.

In his 2017 book *The Fourth Industrial Revolution*, Klaus Schwab, the founder and executive chairman of the World Economic Forum, defined an industrial revolution as 'when new technologies and novel ways of perceiving the world trigger a profound change in economic systems and social structures' (p. 6). The book's premise is that we are currently in the middle of a fourth industrial revolution, and he discusses this in relation to previous industrial revolutions. Let's take a quick look at the different revolutions he identifies.

The first industrial revolution began around 1760 with the development of steam engines and coal, which was fundamental in powering everything from textile manufacturing to agriculture to transportation. Working life was mostly centred around agriculture before the advent of steam power changed everything. Who would have thought that heating water to produce steam would change an entire generation and have such a huge impact on people's lives? On the back of this, metallurgy developed, and powered steamships and railways became the new infrastructure and determined the way people moved from one point to another. It also brought about a new era where cheap factory labour became a new workforce sector. Those who worked in agriculture and were able to learn, adapt or adopt new factory-based skills became the middle class of the economy, and industrialisation thrived. They were the career successes during that era because they adapted their skills to fit the demands of industry.

Then around 1870 the second industrial revolution began, jump-started by the discovery of oil and gas. Even though steam engines were still available, they became old technology as they gave way to petrol engines, and a new method of transportation from one place to another was quickly ushered in. This became the age of aeroplanes and automobiles. Everything started to move faster and faster, and if you were slow and didn't flow or grow with the times, well, your career lost its glow. And with the discovery of oil and gas, the development of dyes, fabric and fertilisers began and there was a science boom. This process may have begun in the laboratories, but before long the factories blossomed, ushering in the industrial age of mass production. Science and development were so fast that they affected the way people worked and separated the urbanites from the villagers. People with the right skills left their homes to work in factories in the cities and earned a lot of money for having skills that aligned with the new era. Then, with the advent of telephones, radio and electricity, the way people communicated and engaged with their societies changed dramatically.

This second revolution continued until the 1960s, when the digital industrial revolution, the third industrial revolution, was born. If you thought the second industrial revolution moved fast, check out what happened in the third. The development of semiconductors, micro-processors, personal computing and the internet changed everything. Miniaturised materials took the world by storm. Analogue systems in electronic and mechanical devices gave way to digital disruptive systems, and global interconnectivity soared. There was a new form of mass production now powered by electronics and automation, and the skills needed to configure and design these connected worlds became in demand. Then nuclear energy was discovered and space research began to grow, as did biotechnology, none of which had been part of the second industrial revolution. It became paramount to acquire skills to meet the challenges of these human intellectual interventions.

Dear reader, welcome to the fourth industrial revolution, the era of impossibilities beyond compare, in which you now live.

As I wrote this book, I was also visualising its cover. I knew it needed to capture the book's essence and showcase the intercon-nectivity between graduate and professional life in some way. When thinking about different designs, three main concepts emerged, and my designer was smart enough to capture them. But then it occurred to me that I could do something different. I could engage my potential readers and ask which design appealed to them most, or if it made more sense to combine concepts from the three designs.

So this is what I did.

I put up a post on LinkedIn showing the three cover concepts, and asked people to let me know which cover concept they preferred and why, or which combination of concepts they would like. Over a one-week period, I had over 10,000 views, and the responses I received formed the basis on which I chose the current book cover. This decision process was only possible because we now live in another industrial era, where the virtual world monitors and steers the physical world. This fourth industrial revolution can therefore be categorised into three main human interventions: the digital, the physical and the biological. The digital represents the age of the cloud, big data and the internet of things (IoT), the physical represents transportation, advanced robotics and 3D printing, while the biological covers interventions in targeted medical solutions and nanotechnology. So think for a minute and ask yourself the question, 'Do my current skills or knowledge align with any of these in full or in part?'

My career is well aligned with the digital era, even though I am continually trying to develop more skills to prepare for now and the future of work. To work out if your skills align with those needed, let's look at the ten skills identified by top think tank Institute for the Future (IFTF) as the most relevant to employers now and in the near future. Irrespective of your career route, for me these are the crucial skills to give you a competitive advantage over your contemporaries.

These are the top ten skills that IFTF think will make you more employable:

1 Sense-Making
2 Social Intelligence
3 Novel and Adaptive Thinking
4 Cross Cultural Competency
5 Computational Thinking
6 New Media Literacy
7 Transdisciplinarity
8 Design Mindset
9 Cognitive Load Management
10 Virtual Collaboration

(Source: Institute for the Future, http://www.iftf.org/futureworkskills/)

CASE STUDY 5: USING THE FOURTH INDUSTRIAL REVOLUTION TO DRIVE YOUR CAREER

Let's take a look at a friend of mine who built his enterprise with a full understanding of the fourth industrial revolution. His name is Kola Aina, and he is founder and chief executive of Ventures Platform Africa. His first degree was in electrical and electronic engineering, even though he really wanted to study something to do with design. In retrospect he says that if he could go back and start his first degree again, he would study computing or economics, the key areas of knowledge that underpin his current work. But as I said above, further education provides you with another opportunity to get it right, and Kola did: he went on to do an MBA, which gave him a sound knowledge of business administration and, more crucially, corporate finance. And so his career grew from corporate strategy to technology entrepreneurship to venture capital, supporting entrepreneurs who display amazing soft skills in their business propositions. Even though he didn't end up working in engineering, he says that the analytical skills he picked up in his first degree drove – and still drive – most of his career activity. When I asked him what his biggest career mistake was, he said, 'Not starting networking earlier, and doing too many things at once.' When I asked him to give young students and professionals a piece of advice, he said eloquently, 'Read widely, volunteer, find alignment between your passion and your work and be comfortable with information technology irrespective of your field of study.' Considering he had never read *The Graduate Code* when he told me this, isn't that just remarkable?

Right away, I can see which skills on this list I am good at. I have developed skills in social and emotional intelligence, adaptive thinking and transdisciplinarity, and I am working on my skills in virtual collaboration and cross-cultural competency, but I really struggle with computational thinking, cognitive load management and design. Being aware of this gives me focus, and enables me to come up with an agenda to prepare me for the future.

To wrap up this section, I urgently need to refer you to an important sector that dominates this new era, one which you most definitely should not ignore from a career perspective.

You remember that each of the first three industrial revolutions had a prevailing energy source – steam in the first, oil and gas in the second and nuclear in the third – but what about the fourth? That's a really good question, don't you think? Well, the energy sources that are most advocated for (and will continue to be most advocated for) are sustainable energy sources that have little or no impact on humans and the planet. I am referring to things like wind, solar, tides and biomass, to mention but a few. As the world has advanced industrially and technologically during the different industrial revolutions, it has placed the globe in a position where it is being stressed and stretched beyond acceptable limits. This pressure has been captured on many different fronts, with the term 'climate change' probably best depicting the fallout from and negative side of industrial revolutions.

For the first time ever, then, mankind is more aware of and interested in the impact of industrial revolutions almost as much as the revolutions themselves, and this has implications for the world of work. An entirely new discipline has been created, known as sustainability, whose focus is on reducing (or at least monitoring) the impact of human intervention and technological advancements on the natural world. With increasing industrialisation across the world, the need for sustainable approaches to waste and pollution management has become crucial. People have finally realised that the wastefulness of our industrial society compromises nature's ability to sustain our needs and the needs of future generations.

In an era where global concerns about sustainability are at a peak – as shown by the current drive by high-level international and national government authorities, large corporations, businesses and the international community to minimise their impact on people and the planet – the graduate career has a role to play, especially in developing economies, where few people have the necessary and appropriate knowledge and skills in this area.

So just as you need to consider how your studies, career or current professional competences align with the three main human interventions of the fourth industrial revolution (physical, digital and biological) and the central skills that power these, you also need to consider how you align with a sustainability agenda. A good place to start is by looking at the Sustainable Development Goals (SDGs) set by the United Nations. In 2015, after substantial deliberations with 193 member states, the UN launched 17 SDGs, with 169 targets between them as an agenda for transforming our world by 2030. These were agreed as follows:

- SDG 1: No poverty
- SDG 2: Zero hunger
- SDG 3: Good health and well-being
- SDG 4: Quality education
- SDG 5: Gender equality
- SDG 6: Clean water and sanitation
- SDG 7: Affordable and clean energy
- SDG 8: Decent work and economic growth
- SDG 9: Industry, innovation and infrastructure
- SDG 10: Reduced inequalities
- SDG 11: Sustainable cities and communities
- SDG 12: Responsible production and consumption
- SDG 13: Climate action
- SDG 14: Life below water
- SDG 15: Life on land
- SDG 16: Peace, justice and strong institutions
- SDG 17: Partnerships for the goals

(Source: https://www.un.org/sustainabledevelopment/
sustainable-development-goals/)

Though they are listed as separate goals, they are inextricably linked – and rightly so, as you cannot totally deal with challenges in isolation. To engage with challenges and opportunities in context, you need a holistic approach. The 17 goals also show universality and a potential for transformation if well appropriated.

It therefore makes sense to think about how in some sense your career promotes, has an impact on or is impacted upon by one or more of these goals. For instance, I can see how my career relates to several of these: I did a doctorate in environmental management, work in consulting for universities, support young people and advise African governments. Already I can see that my career is well aligned with SDGs 4, 6, 7, 12, 13, 16 and 17. The next thing for me is to prioritise which key goals form the core of what I do career-wise. And if you ask me which of these goals is my top priority, I can confidently say that it is SDG 17 – partnerships for the goals. At the beginning of this book I referred to myself as the navigator and connector, because I am all about building strategic sustainable partnerships in order to increase Africa's prosperity.

It is important to note that irrespective of your field of study or professional space, you can include sustainability within what you do. We now have terms like green accounting, green banking, green branding, green construction, green consulting, green education, green enterprise, green manufacturing, green procurement, sustainable financing, sustainable infrastructure and so on to show a new range of career options which consider impact in one form or another. (It is worth noting that the terms 'green' and 'sustainable' are usually interchangeable.) Although you don't have to specialise in a core sustainability area, you do need to know how your career activity impacts on or aligns either with particular sustainable development goals or with sustainability more generally.

CASE STUDY 6: INCREASING YOUR KNOWLEDGE OF ONE AREA WHILE WORKING IN ANOTHER

I am reminded here of another good friend of mine, Mr Stan Deh, a top banker from Ghana. Stan did his first degree in administration and graduated with a BSc. He quickly went into a career in banking and finance, which he absolutely loved. (I must say that he was probably more prepared than those, such as my friend Anthony Aggreh, who chose to work in banking because it is the only thing both available and well-paid. I will come back to Anthony at the end of this chapter.) Stan ended up becoming a marketer of banking products, and so to increase his competence in the area he undertook a master's degree in e-commerce and marketing. Surprise, surprise! This gave him the much-needed intellectual and professional capacity to do his work effectively. And how he soared, soon becoming head of public-sector retail banking at Stanbic Bank, one of the largest banks in Ghana. Well, things soon took a refreshingly new turn after I recommended he consider aligning his career with global sustainability. 'But I am in banking,' he said, wondering how banking and sustainability were linked. (As you know by now, there are always links, and you can find them with guidance.) Anyway, Stan took the plunge. How did he do it? He increased his knowledge of sustainability while continuing to work in traditional banking. Remember that I mentioned the value of short courses in Chapter 15? Well, Stan went on a spree, taking courses that increased his knowledge and skills. To date, he has gained the following certifications from short courses:
- Business Sustainability Management (from the Institute of Sustainable Leadership, University of Cambridge, UK)
- Certified Expert in Microinsurance (Frankfurt University, Germany)
- Certified Expert in Climate Adaptation Finance (Frankfurt University, Germany)

- Certificate in Renewable Energy Management and Finance (European Energy Centre)
- Solar Project Development Programme – Ghana (GIZ, Germany, PI Institute and Mittelstand Global)

Now I find Stan's passion impressive and his resolve impeccable. Even I didn't know that the above courses were available until he told me. And before you complain that he is a banker and can afford to do expensive courses, Stan emphasised that it was his passion to be relevant in his area that drove him to search for these courses and apply for them. (Besides, courses don't have to cost a lot; there are many free courses available, which you won't be aware of until you search for them.) Currently, Stan, as part of a new team, leads a sustainable banking agenda for the Central Bank of Ghana and has created a new relevant career niche on the back of his current role.

I will cover the process of specialisation a little more in the next chapter. But for now, let me balance it with another case study.

CASE STUDY 7: FINDING YOUR NICHE WITHIN A CAREER CHOSEN FOR ITS CONVENIENCE

You still remember my friend and brother, Anthony Aggreh? Of course you do. Unlike Stan, Anthony dabbled in banking for convenience (rather than because it was his passion) after graduating with a first degree in chemistry. You may be wondering now what connection chemistry has with banking. Well, there may be one somewhere, but in this case there was absolutely nothing to link the two. Anthony just saw a job there for the taking. And like Stan, he soared in banking. An impressive and hard-working guy, he moved up the ranks quickly, but soon found a great love aligning his banking career with a sustainable agenda.

He also started independent study, attending a series of several seminars and workshops, and before long became involved in a new-found niche – sustainable finance, a sector in which he now thrives in Nigeria. To showcase his drive to become an authority in the field, he is now about to undertake a postgraduate programme in sustainable finance for major projects with a specialisation in chemically driven energy sources, which takes him back to the knowledge acquired in his first degree. This goes to show that knowledge is never truly lost, and that everything you do empowers you to become that career professional you must become.

Let's move on to Activity 19 now, and consider how you can align your skills with those needed in the current industrial age and beyond.

ACTIVITY 19

19a. Which one of the three broad human interventions within the fourth industrial revolution do your current career skills and knowledge most align with? The digital, the physical or the biological? (If it is a combination of more than one of the three, also state this clearly.)

19b. Which of the ten listed skills for the future do you currently have, and which do you know you lack?

19c. List which of the 17 United Nations Sustainable Development Goals your current career skills and knowledge align with. (If your answer is 'none', highlight which of these SDGs you could most align yourself with as you progress in your studies or career.)

19d. Search online to find out about some sustainable career pathways within your current studies or career direction which you didn't know about before now. Try and capture these in half a page.

19e. In 19b you listed the knowledge and skills you currently lack. Using the internet, find out about three currently available short courses you could take to change this. Write these down.

19f. Using the internet, find out about three available short courses you could take to increase your knowledge and skills around sustainability. Write these down.

NOTES

NOTES

CHAPTER 20

Optimising opportunities for internationals

· ·

THE TENETS

20.1 If the change is in your hands, you mustn't struggle through your studies or work in an environment with minimal career support and still face the same struggle in one with enough support.

20.2 In a globally connected world in which connectivity is the most valued currency, you need to always think local and act global.

· ·

At the early stages of conceptualising the writing of this book, I always knew that the positioning of my piece was unique. The book's primary aim was to bring important information to the African career space using lessons learnt from my experiences in the United Kingdom. It was almost as if I had stood up and could see clearly why some things worked and why others didn't unless they were adapted, or adopted differently. That unique position of being caught in the middle between a developing and somewhat underdeveloped economy and a developed one comes with some interesting perspectives.

In this chapter, I am taking a step back to focus a little more on those who are studying, living and working overseas. In other words, an international is a person who has left their country to study and work and who probably now lives overseas. I will use the United Kingdom as a sample overseas destination here, but am sure you can draw appropriate parallels with any other overseas study and working destinations. Regardless of where you study and work, the proposed premise remains valid, I believe, and I intend to explore this shortly. (You could perhaps use the word 'foreigner' in place of 'international', but I use that term advisedly and with respect for political correctness.)

First let me paint you a picture of the big challenges I faced as a student when I first came to the UK to study, and hopefully this will set the scene to explore the opportunities for students, young graduates and professionals considering studying overseas.

Firstly, as mentioned in previous chapters, I had to learn to cope with the disparity between dependence on and independence from tutors. In Nigeria, as in most African countries, a student has an almost total dependence on their lecturers and tutors. As I discussed earlier in this book, lecturers load you with lecture notes and mostly leave little breathing space for independent thinking or creative reasoning. There is a colloquial term in many African countries, 'garbage in, garbage out', which, though a computing analogy, is used to describe when in examinations a student gives back to the lecturer exactly what they were fed in class. In fact, in some cases, the apparent demonstration of intellect and the sign of a great student is how consistently he or she is able to garbage out the garbage that has gone in. That is the African study environment which I grew up in, where the lecturer was lord and master and ruled the intellectual empire with a rod of creativity-starving iron.

So imagine my despair when a lecturer walks into class during my postgraduate programme in the UK and, part-way through the lecture, stops and asks us, 'So what do *you* think about this scenario?' Alarm bells went off in my head. I thought to myself, 'This is abominable – lecturers aren't allowed to ask me my opinions.' As far as I was concerned, all I was used to was lecturers telling me what to think. After all, that had been good enough for me, because each time I had parroted back to them what they had taught me in the first place, I did amazingly in my examinations. (And yes, that reminds me, I grew up in an examinations-only-driven environment where writing reports, essays and case study analyses were almost alien concepts. Imagine my struggle when I now had to write essay upon essay with word limits, cross references, plagiarism screenings and independent recommendations. Oh, how much I struggled. But soon I found that when I was given a chance to explore my creativity, I flew, and flew fast.

I had grown up in a culture where I wasn't allowed to call a professor by name unless I used the title 'Professor' before it, or else the academic gods would rain down fire and brimstone on me (figuratively speaking, of course!). However, back in the UK it was the opposite, and indeed sometimes caused mild offence if I used the title. I had to address all my professors by their first names. I remember having to remind myself each time I did so that this was okay. Who wouldn't, especially when your previous experiences were of fire and brimstone? A better way to paint this picture, I think, is to show you a typical UK examination marking scheme. (I have decided to focus on grading from 50% scoring and above for illustration, as anything below this is considered a fail.)

African students will immediately see the big difference in marks awarded to innovative thinking versus garbage in, garbage out, and this is why I struggled to score above 65% during my postgraduate degree in the UK. To score 90% and above, you had to show original thinking and perspectives argued logically and reasonably.

TYPICAL MARKING CRITERIA IN UK UNIVERSITIES

90-100%	As below, but also original perspectives or insights, argued logically.	
80-89%	As below, but also evidence of extensive reading of sources given by the lecturer but extending the breadth of the lecture material.	Marks in this boundary worthy of a distinction
70-79%	Accurate and complete, demonstrating understanding in depth and draws upon extensive reading of the source of the lecture material. Well ordered, using good English, appropriate examples and plenty of illustrative information.	
65-69%	Comprehensive, although not complete. Showing understanding based on an ability to marshal information and to support arguments with appropriate examples. Good English. Some pieces of information or examples go beyond the lecture material in either depth or breadth.	Marks in this boundary worthy of a merit
60-64%	As above, but either occasionally lacking accuracy or with few examples	
55-59%	Concise but accurate. Based largely on lecture material. Information presented clearly but lacking any originality.	Marks in this boundary worthy of a pass
50-54%	As above, but with occasional lapses of accuracy or logic.	

Now the way examinations are marked in each of these two countries is connected with cultural differences, and this is okay, but did the way I was taught in Africa have an impact on my career progression in that space? Absolutely, and this leads me to another point. The effect of the study environment in Africa was such that not only did I come to depend on my lecturers' every word, but – and most importantly – I learnt to expect little in terms of academic or career support from the university system or administration. This is the reason I emphasised in Chapter 3, 'Taking the bull by the horns', that you need to take your career growth into your own hands, or else you will falter and fail.

Now, is it possible that people who are conditioned not to rely on the system struggle when they come into an environment with good support systems in place? After speaking with several international offices and academic support departments of UK universities and conversations with several hundreds of international students from Africa, there is a clear case of support systems being available but international students failing to take advantage of them. (That includes me, by the way, because I cannot remember going to the career support department of my university at any point during my master's degree or PhD in the UK.) Isn't that astounding?

To be fair, international and student support offices in UK universities are generally great at what they do, especially in terms of providing careers advice, guidance and direction. What they are less good at is providing advice and direction to international students who want to return to their home countries after their studies. They can give generic career advice, but that is about it. Most don't know enough about overseas career situations and job markets to guide international students who want to return to work or set up enterprises in their home countries after their studies. This was certainly my situation. So in some sense I had to take the bull by the horns, even in the UK. It's almost as if the situation in most African universities – where there are not enough academic career support systems in place – is mirrored in overseas institutions for African students despite all the support systems in place. A bit of a double whammy, don't you think?

Rather surprisingly (and perhaps understandably), I noticed that most international students suddenly get panicky about what they will do next career-wise, and start looking into their options only weeks before the end of their programmes in the UK. This is when many make very rushed and confused career decisions that place them in an even worse position than before they arrived overseas. This is when some naively decide to do a PhD after their master's degree as a way to extend their time before seeking employment, even if they are not prepared for the rigorous work it involves. Some just take another master's degree as if that will resolve their confusion. Some are just not ready to return to their home country, especially when they have not figured out their career direction. The successful ones are those who know exactly what they wish to get out of studying overseas and how they will use this after they finish their studies. This was the case for Lily Mburu, a young Kenyan lady who studied law in her first degree. She states clearly that studying for her master's degree in law in the UK was to expand her world view, test her resolve and reaffirm her purpose. She always knew that she wanted to return to her home country after her master's degree, and that is exactly what she did. After a stint at a charity organisation, exploring her enthusiasm for human rights, she soon settled in academia, which she describes as her passion and career forte. Studying overseas is the best career decision she ever made, she declares with confidence. I wonder how many of you can say that?

I would like to ask you a question here: how can you struggle in an unsupportive environment, then spend a lot of money on international tuition fees to study in an environment with lots of support available, and still finish your programme having accessed no support?

When you have a lot of support available and don't take advantage of it, you have no one but yourself to blame. So in line with the different chapters of this book, it makes sense to highlight the support that is available when you are studying or living overseas. As I already mentioned, I will assume the UK is your study destination when painting this picture.

So let's start with student societies. There are many societies to choose from at UK universities, and even if your programme takes up a lot of your time, try and join (and be active in!) one that interests you.

Volunteering is a big deal overseas, especially in the UK. Many people are inspired to start a charity organisation, while others feel inspired to volunteer for an existing charity. Remember what I talked about in Chapter 8, 'Working for no pay'? Take advantage of the opportunity to volunteer, pick up relevant skills and experience and build your CV. You need to consciously seek and deliver on this before you realise that your programme is about to come to an end and you have not achieved anything.

One thing that overseas universities – well, at least in the UK – are quite good at is engagement with industry. For instance, I mentioned before that the Environment Centre at Lancaster University has over 24 environmental SMEs resident in its Enterprise and Business Partnerships unit. So take advantage of these opportunities, and engage with the relevant companies based in your universities. I remember that before I completed my PhD, I had signed several Memorandums of Understanding with different companies that I wanted to work with for the African market. At this stage, I had experienced my light-bulb moment and I knew exactly what I wanted to do after my studies. (Besides, I had restrictions on the number of hours I was allowed to work as an international student but didn't have the same restrictions on the number of MOUs or agreements I could sign.) So, ladies and gentlemen, go to town on those engagements and agreements.

I have spoken a lot about networking and building your affiliations, and I see no better environment to develop global networks than in overseas universities. Among other things, these reputable institutions measure their international status by the number of international students they attract, as I'm sure you remember. And therein lies the opportunity.

If you combine international tuition fees with accommodation and subsistence fees, flights, visas, clothing and all, do you realise how expensive it is to study overseas, particularly compared to studying in your home country, especially if you come from a developing economy? Bearing in mind the cost of overseas study, then, any international student you see on campus is likely to fall into one of three categories: firstly, they might be rich or well to do, with wealthy or influential parents who can afford to send them overseas to be educated; secondly, they might be on some kind of scholarship, meaning that they are of above-average intelligence; or thirdly, they might be paying for their own study. The third type of student doesn't necessarily need to be rich to fund themselves, but they must be driven and passionate enough to consider an overseas education important enough to pay for. If you think about it, you are studying alongside many people who have the potential to help you achieve your career objectives. What better than to get to know as many people as possible while studying?

Most international students tend to want to associate themselves with students of similar backgrounds and national inclinations, and maybe even from the same country. This is totally natural and okay. However, remember that you might lose a huge opportunity to build a global career network while you are studying overseas if you do not make strategic efforts to find out who other people are and where they are from. What is the point of studying at an international university if by the end of your studies you are not an internationally connected graduate? In a globally connected world in which connectivity is one of the most valued currencies, you need to think and act global.

A good starting point is to take a quick trip to your university's international student office to ask how many international students are studying there and where they are from geographically or regionally. This at least will arm you with information about the global representations within that academic space and help you plan a strategy to engage and build an incredible network of graduate associates who could have an impact on your professional career after you finish your studies. Have you noticed how much China is investing in Africa? Did you just stumble into the daughter of the chief executive of a big Chinese investment corporation and not even notice her? Even though you are African, you can still find a way to attend some China-related events and activities on and off campus. Maybe you are studying a programme in media. Might you have walked past the son or daughter of the CEO of the largest media conglomerate in East Africa every day without even realising it? Imagine now that you are from West Africa and wish to return there after you finish your studies, and you have the right skills and capacity this media conglomerate requires for its next regional expansion – into West Africa. Do you get my drift here?

If you are already a graduate, another good step is to contact the alumni office of your alma mater and ask what events they are putting on and what services they have available for alumni. You would be surprised how much they have to offer you. They hold alumni seminars, networking sessions, career talks, business forums and more. For me, engaging with other alumni is a good way to make up for the opportunities you lost while you were a student. But if you don't engage, you will not gain leverage.

I highlighted the need to learn outside the box in Chapter 9, and there is no better time to do this than when studying, living or working overseas. This is because most international universities regularly offer a wide range of short professional courses, skills development seminars, career-enhancing workshops and global network-enhancing events in and around campus.

The truth here is that unless you are particularly conscious of the need to attend these, you are unlikely to do so. It is more likely that you will get so preoccupied with your degree modules and endless essay- and report-writing that you don't notice that the same lecturer who teaches a course in Management 105 also runs a short free course every weekend on how to deliver the best PowerPoint presentation. Notice here I said free! Courses like these are nearly all free of charge. By the end of my PhD in environmental management, I had undertaken over 20 short professional courses, most of which had nothing to do with environmental management – and why would they need to if I was already doing a PhD in that subject? I have certificates in manual handling, safe handling of medicines, first aid, health and safety in the workplace, project management, enterprise development, and so on, all of which I wouldn't normally study as part of my main course. What these courses do is give you leverage to be flexible, adaptable and adventurous in your career progression and open up opportunities to navigate different routes if you need to.

If you have already graduated but still live and work overseas, there is a good chance that you live within walking distance of a university. Well, you need to keep up your association with that university, because it contains your opportunity to engage with a reputable organisation, grow your global networks and increase your skills and capacities while you figure out your next career action. My point is simple. A university always remains relevant to you whether you are a student, a young graduate or a professional. Get the best from it.

So now let's look at Activity 20, and think about how you could get the most out of an international university.

. . . .

ACTIVITY 20

Investigate and engage with the relevant unit of an international university and find out the following:

20a. Which student societies and bodies have a different cultural or professional background from yours.

20b. What relevant professional courses are available that are different from your main course of study.

20c. What the careers office does and what services they have for international graduates.

20d. What programmes/initiatives the alumni office has for international graduates.

20e. Which department(s) manages engagement with companies, and what opportunities students/alumni have to engage with these companies.

20f. What volunteer opportunities there are at the university for international graduates and how you could get involved.

CASE STUDY 8: NAVIGATING A CAREER AS AN INTERNATIONAL GRADUATE

One really great example of career navigation, particularly for an international graduate, comes from my good friend Griselda Togobo, a lovely Ghanaian lady and incredible role model. Seriously, this lady is impressive. Okay, check this out. Griselda did her first degree in Ghana, in electrical and electronic engineering. According to her, studying engineering provided her with the analytical and problem-solving skills she now enjoys in her career. Then she proceeded to do a master's degree in industrial systems, manufacture and management at Cambridge University. Guess what she did next? She then joined a professional services firm and trained as a chartered accountant specialising in auditing. Now have you worked out the twist? She specialised in the financial aspects of the engineering and manufacturing sectors. It might have originally sounded risky, but it was all in the plan. And what does Griselda do now? She now runs one of the most reputable female empowerment powerhouse consultancies in the UK, Forward Ladies, and consults for big corporations about their gender equality capacity-building programmes, with a strong emphasis on promoting women in sciences and engineering. When I asked her what her biggest career mistakes had been, she said with a smile, 'Not realising the importance of networks early enough, not planning early enough to create a niche for myself, and forgetting how much value I bring to anything I do.' Griselda advocates for career mentorship, taking the career bull by the horns in your youthful prime and simply refusing to take no for an answer. She sounds like someone who gets the Graduate Code, don't you think?

NOTES

NOTES

CHAPTER 21

Understanding and planning your space

. . . .

THE TENETS

21.1   The mark of a successful career is that you enjoy what you do and that whatever it is fulfils a need and gives value to you, someone or something else, whether you are paid for it or not.

21.2   Whatever you do in your career, understand and appreciate your strategic place but never restrict your impact space.

. . . .

Well, isn't this exciting? You have nearly reached the end of *The Graduate Code*.

This chapter hopes to wrap things up, beginning with the ultimate question: how do you determine career success? At what point can you say that you are having, or have had, a successful career? What does 'career success' even mean? Now that last one is a really difficult question to answer, but there is an answer nonetheless, even if it differs from one person to the next. Some might think that earning a million pounds a year is the true hallmark of a successful career. Others might be fulfilled in their career by putting a thousand smiles on the faces of poor children in a village in Malawi.

Success is really subjective, but you need to figure out how you will define it – and soon, too. Although one person's career success is not the same as another's, I will try to capture what I think it means.

So to me, you can be said to be a 'career success' if you enjoy what you do and whatever it is fulfils a need and gives value to someone or something else. Whether you are paid for it or not is a different thing entirely. And in some sense, what you are paid for it could be the evidence of the value your role creates for you and gives to others. I like to call this the *career push and pull phenomenon*.

Let me see if I can explain this further. I use *push* in the sense that you have the right environment and resources to give something out – a skill, knowledge, a solution, a product, a service, a word – and you enjoy giving this out. You are the one pushing that interesting thing you have to give. *Pull* refers to a market need, a demand, a challenge, a problem, confusion, despair, issues which require your help to be resolved. This gives your role value. If you enjoy what you do, the more demand there will be for what you offer and the more you will want to give. This is the career push and pull phenomenon. This, ladies and gentlemen, is the foundation on which that career grows. It is when what you can give (or are already giving) complements what is needed or in demand.

Now there are two things most likely to frustrate career growth, and they are these.

Firstly, you may struggle to find the right platform or environment to express the value you can give (and most importantly enjoy giving) when you need to. This is the quintessential terminator of career growth. In this kind of situation you have a lot of skills and expertise to give (push), but you simply cannot give them because they aren't needed in the work you are doing. You hear of people saying, 'I love my job, but I could do so much more with my life.' This creates a limitation in the push element.

The second major factor that can limit your career growth is not getting the right value from what you are giving. In cases like this, you are in the right environment to give all that you can give – and in some cases you do give it all – but you are not properly appreciated for it. So you hear people say things like 'I love my job but the pay is rubbish/morale is low/it has become just a routine.' Inherently, there is a limitation in the pull element: there is nothing strong enough there to make you want to keep giving what you have.

Now different people have different pushes and pulls, and you need to think about what yours are. To work these out, try asking yourself questions like 'What is your interpretation of career success?', 'What floats your boat?' or 'What would make you wake up in the morning with a smile on your face because it is time to go to work?' Once you figure out what you have and can give (your push) and what you want to get from giving that thing you have (your pull), then you have started creating what your career space will look like.

For me, owning a consultancy with a thousand members of staff was never going to be my thing. Even though I have been running a consulting firm for many years, I always knew that I didn't want to head up a huge corporation because I had to balance it with other things that I loved. I knew that doing charity work, connecting people, places and processes, inspiring young people and empowering women and girls were core activities that brought me the most career satisfaction (my pulls). So whatever I have done, I have sought these things out and achieved them by giving talks, consulting, running social media campaigns, and now writing (my push factors). I have never been motivated by the amount in my bank account.

To be honest, having a lot of money is fantastic if it enables me to align with my pushes and pulls. However, if there was very little in my bank account and I could still deliver these career objectives, I absolutely would. I hope that makes sense. So ask yourself again what floats your boat. If you know this, you will be able to judge when you are starting to achieve your career successes.

All the above captures your theoretical or conceptual career space. But what about your geographical career space? To work this out, I will rephrase another question: how do you determine where you should operate in your career? If you are Tanzanian and studying, living and working in Tanzania, does it mean that Tanzania alone is your career space? If you work as a researcher in a local public university in Mali, does that mean that Mali is your career space? If you are studying in the United States of America, do you know what your career space covers?

Obviously when I ask these questions I am assuming that at this stage, after going through the different elements of the Graduate Code, you at least have a sense of what you might want to do. In the worst-case scenario you know what your career should or could look like. Whether you are wanting to go into or remain in employment, start your own new enterprise or grow a current business, or just want to study overseas to get the right knowledge for something new and exciting, there is something powerful about knowing your space.

I am going to be asking a lot of questions here, so stick with me please. Imagine if you knew that even though you live in Angola now, you could get a job in Norway. Imagine if you knew that even though you run a small company in downtown Lagos, Nigeria, you could provide services to clients in Lusaka, Zambia. Imagine if you knew that even though you sold your products to folks in Dar es Salaam, Tanzania, there was a ready market waiting for you in Kigali, Rwanda, an hour's flight away. Why is this important when you are framing your career direction? Well, imagine you were early in your research career, working in a private university in Zimbabwe, and knew that there was a demand for your research in six other African countries. How do you think this might affect your career positioning and outlook on opportunities?

For a very long time, Nigeria was my only career space. I didn't know anything about any other country, neither did I visit any. I sought my first job in Nigeria and when I decided to set up my own company, the focus was also Nigeria. In fact, when I set up my non-governmental organisation in the UK (the Xn Foundation), supporting Nigerian students was also the focus (no doubt you remember that the first programme we developed was called the International Conference of Nigerian Students). It was all about Nigeria, and Nigeria alone. Over time, I realised that restricting my career space restricted my options and my career growth had a ceiling.

So while you might start from a single geographical space, think carefully about what new spaces you might occupy. So Nigeria is a big country with a population of over 180 million people, but the moment you consider that Africa has over a billion people, then Nigeria suddenly feels small. Think about that for a minute, and right away you see your reach is higher. You remember I told you that you should aim to give value within your career? Well, there is no way I can talk about value without talking about challenges. So let's look at some of those.

Some five years ago, when I first began travelling to different African countries, I tended to notice that the number of Africans on each flight was greater than the number of non-Africans (at least, that is what I assumed based on the colour of passengers' skin). As the years progressed, the reverse started becoming true. I remember taking a flight from Amsterdam to Nairobi and approximately 90% of the passengers were non-Africans. So I started asking myself what all these people kept going to Africa for. When you ask an average non-African about Africa, you tend to hear statements like 'It's such a beautiful continent, full of resources and opportunities, and wealth is in abundance, just like poverty is.' However, when you ask the average African living in Africa about their home continent, what you are more likely to hear is, 'Oh, things don't work, the government is useless, I need to leave this continent and travel overseas.'

It would seem to me that non-Africans know something about Africa that Africans do not. Well, maybe they can just see things more clearly from an unconnected, non-conflicted and unbiased plane. But then let's focus on what many Africans actually see. Many Africans see challenges, but perhaps they don't see enough challenges, because when people see more challenges, the pull factor tends to be stronger as the value you can bring is greater. The more challenges there are, the more opportunities there are. Because Africa is the continent with the biggest challenges, it also has the biggest opportunities. So what challenges are we talking about in Africa? Let's check out a few.

One of the major challenges facing the continent, according to UK Aid, is that over 600 million people in sub-Saharan Africa do not have access to electricity. That's more than 60% of the population. Over 50% of businesses view this lack of access to electricity as a major constraint to doing business, and so power outages cost African countries about 2% of their annual GDP.

Another challenge is water and sanitation. About 57 million Nigerians, 3 million Ghanaians and 17 million Kenyans do not have access to clean and safe water, and over 60% of the population of most African countries do not have access to improved sanitation, according to estimates from Water Aid.

Then there are issues around illicit use of resources. The Natural Capital Coalition calculates that Africa loses over £150 billion of its natural capital annually through illicit financial flows, illegal mining, illegal logging, illegal trade in wildlife, unregulated fishing, environmental degradation and loss.

Food shortages are a major problem as well: in February 2017, famine was declared in areas of South Sudan, affecting other countries in the region, and this was the first time in around six years that famine had been declared anywhere in the world.

Finally, waste presents a huge challenge. According to a World Bank Urban Development Series Report, Africa currently produces in excess of 70 million tonnes of waste yearly, and with rapid urbanisation and growing economies it is projected that this figure will exceed 160 million tonnes of waste by 2025. Meanwhile, less than 10% of this waste is recycled or reused.

In addition to all these major problems, according to business advice website Smallstarter (www.smallstarter.com), of the 25 poorest countries in the world, only four of them are not in Africa, and the skills gap created as a result of gender inequality, which I discussed in Chapter 16, costs Africa in excess of 100 billion USD yearly.

I have given figures above for electricity access, water and sanitation, natural capital, food and waste, poverty and the cost of the skills gap, and already the African picture looks really grim. Imagine if I went on to look in more detail at other areas – I think I would need to write another book just to capture these challenges. Having said that, I do intend to write another book to capture the huge challenges and opportunities in Africa from the insights of a travelling African expert. (I mean me!)

Anyway, let's focus on the opportunities, because there are many.

According to the Africa Competitiveness Report 2017, put together by the World Economic Forum, the African Development Bank and the World Bank Group, Africa is currently undergoing an economic renaissance, having experienced an average growth rate of more than 5% in the last decade. Put into perspective, other continents of the world struggled over the same period, growing less than 2% on average. With over 1 billion people on the continent, projected in the report to hit 1.5 billion by 2030, 2.5 billion by 2050 (surpassing China) and putting population figures on a par with Asia by 2100, Africa is a powerhouse of human capital the world cannot afford to take for granted.

And guess what, the world is not taking Africa for granted at all. (I don't want to get stuck talking about Africa and its grandeur, because I won't be able to stop!) You notice that all of a sudden the grim picture I painted above starts to pale into insignificance. It's all about perspective, and this is a great way to look at your graduate career.

So the big question now is, 'What African challenge is your graduate career trying to (or able to) solve or provide value to?' How relevant are you, or will you be, in your space? Within the scope of these challenges, what do you – or can you – bring to the table to make a difference? It's probably easier to think about these questions in the form of what product/service, process, policy, partnership or person you can bring.

It's funny, because I really struggle now to compose a strategy, programme or service and not think 'Africa' from the outset. Nigeria has become too small in the grand scheme of things. I reach for the skies and sometimes I touch the ceiling, but that's okay because in my mind I see beyond what I feel. What do you see?

The final aspect of career spaces I would like to touch on briefly is what I like to call your *sectoral career space*. This basically refers to the industry or economic sector in which you have built – or are trying to build – your career.

If you have never considered your sectoral career space, you really should. Generally, the challenge you aim to provide a solution for tells you the sector(s) you should focus on. Remember the African challenges I highlighted around electricity, water, food, waste and natural capital? All these are economic sectors in their own

CASE STUDY 9: IDENTIFYING A CHALLENGE AND USING IT TO DRIVE INNOVATION

One great example of someone putting these thoughts into action is a gentleman who saw the challenges in health and created a product that is changing lives for the better at the moment. Meet Dr Femi Ogunremi, a great Nigerian mind and friend.

Femi studied medicine in Nigeria and travelled to the UK to work, during which period he took several extra continuous professional development programmes, especially in medical education and leadership and public health management. It was after one of these training courses that he started his own company in Nigeria, Monitor Healthcare Ltd. The purpose of this was for him to bring back the knowledge and experience he had gained back to Africa and to give back to the community that had invested so much in him. (You can probably see why he is my friend, right?) He began in employment, working for the National Health Service in England – where he still works – but a spark of enterprise was born, and he has only one goal: to meet the challenges of providing affordable healthcare in Africa. His pull was clear, and he has enough push to jump-start the process. Do you know what he did first? He developed a mobile app and started to bridge the communication gaps in healthcare access. Remember the top ten career skills identified by the Institute for the Future, which I talked about in Chapter 19? Even a multi-award-winning medical doctor like Femi needed new skills and knowledge to stay relevant. For someone with no knowledge of information technology, he found a way to navigate this discipline, and through learning and sheer guts things have picked up significantly. Nigeria was his pilot stage, but Africa remained his career space. What is *your* career space?

right. Surely you have heard of the water industry? Food industry? Electricity and energy industry? That's what I mean by sectoral career spaces. In most cases, you develop an affinity for a sector just because you have worked in that sector for a long time. You have worked in banking for ten years, so all you know about is the banking sector, or you specialise in construction and it becomes your main sector.

As you progress in your career – or, if you are a student, maybe as you start to develop it – what is important is to be aware that you need to be flexible and adaptable to different sectors. It is therefore best to consider other sectors that you could potentially play in. Once you have done that, figure out what aligns your current sector with the new one you are considering, because navigating between one and the other becomes both easier and fulfilling. Some sectoral career navigations (moving from one to another) happen organically and are sometimes unplanned. But guess what? It is even better if you have thought carefully and planned for them.

Planning how you could move into different sectors means that you can divert and direct your energy, resources and skills to growing your expertise in what really interests you. The trouble is that when you are within a single career sector space, you are bound by that space, even if you totally enjoy your work. The potential for career fatigue is low if you can navigate between spaces but retain your core career objectives and offer. Let me give you an example, if I may.

What I do is connect people and places, so I shouldn't be bounded by a sector in the real sense of the word. This means I can (and indeed I am able to) connect anyone in any industry. But on the back of connecting people and places, I build the capacity, skills and knowledge of the people and places I connect so that they become sustainable. This, in a nutshell, is my career objective. But I could do this in any sector, couldn't I? Of course, but for the sake of focus I have narrowed down my sectoral career space into four from the hundreds of possibilities. In order of priority, these four are:

- Education (my core driver)
- Environment (powered by my training/degrees)
- Extractive (powered by my long-term work experiences)
- Entertainment Media (powered by my passion/hobbies).

I like to call these my 4Es Career Sectoral Spaces. They weren't originally linked, but over time I have managed to align them, meaning that the scope of my challenges – and by implication my opportunities – has increased. So I focus on local content in the extractive sector (oil, gas and minerals), which basically means developing the skills and capacity of local suppliers and staff to manage their own natural resources more effectively. I hold seminars, workshops and conferences in the environmental space in an attempt to increase the knowledge and skills of people in different African countries and connect them with each other and with the international community. I have written a book to increase the capacity of young people to improve their career and skills. You see how they are all nicely linked? This way I don't feel like I am doing too many disconnected things, and for me that keeps my focus and specialisation.

Maybe your main driver is a single sectoral space and you should only operate in that area, but at least let it influence other spaces. To give you an example, a friend of mine, Mayra Pereira, a Mozambican professional, has made environmental management her core career space. With a bachelor's and a master's degree in environmental and geographical sciences from a Mozambican and South African university, she spent time as an employee influencing conservation, manufacturing, NGOs, academia and other sectoral spaces. Soon she felt that she needed more influence and control, so she and a friend launched her environmental consulting services company, GreenLight, in Mozambique. When I asked her what advice she had for young students and graduates, she replied, 'Get a mentor, go to networking events, believe in yourself and don't be afraid to make mistakes, as you learn so much in the process.' Isn't that fantastic advice just a perfect illustration of the tenets of the Graduate Code?

Now it's time to move to Activity 21 and think about how you would define success and what potential career spaces are the right ones for you.

· ·

ACTIVITY 21

21a. Project into the future and say what for you would be a successful career? Can you identify your push (what you can give) and your pull (what is in demand) within that career?

21b. What is your current geographical career space? What new geographical career spaces are you considering? And what do you consider your ultimate geographical career space, and why?

21c. What is your current sectoral career space? What new sector(s) are you considering? And what do you consider your top three sectoral spaces of influence?

NOTES

NOTES

....

....

....

....

....

....

....

....

....

....

....

....

....

....

....

....

....

....

....

....

....

....

CHAPTER 22

Conclusion: living by the Graduate Code

. . . .

THE TENETS

22.1   A code is given to be decoded, understood and applied.

22.2   Probe, prioritise, plan and push until you get the ultimate career good.

22.3   In every professional is a student wanting to learn and in every student is a professional waiting to earn. This is the ultimate graduate code.

. . . .

A good driver gets up, gets in their car and drives brilliantly, and most times doesn't even need to think about how to drive. They have driven so often that it has become second nature, and what makes them a good driver is that they live by the Highway Code, among other things. All industry sectors are guided by some sort of rules and regulations which you must comply with or live by. Everything is guided by rules, else there would be chaos. You must have heard of the rules of engagement in war, the laws of nature and physics, the code of ethics and malpractice. Things that have the potential for chaos always seem to have rules that put them in some degree of agreement and alignment.

Well, does the graduate life have the potential for chaos? Are misfortunes and unplanned disturbances part of professional life? Are graduates currently misguided and misinformed? Your answers to these questions give credence to the need for the Graduate Code. It can remain a set of tenets in a book, but the tenets will make no difference to your life if that is all they are. A code is made to be cracked, understood and applied.

As I wrap up this book, I cannot help but remember a situation that sprung up on me a few years ago, one of those things that reminds me to live by what I preach and stay influenced by the tenets of the Graduate Code itself. It was the story of how I came to get involved in the production of one of the best indigenous movies ever made and produced in Africa by Africans. You will remember me referring to myself as a supporter and advocate of female empowerment and gender equality, but what I didn't tell you was what first evoked that passion in me.

What drove my passion to actively support female empowerment was my involvement in the production of the multi-award-winning movie *Dry*, written, directed and produced by the amazing Stephanie Linus (nee Okereke). And I'm sure you probably wondered why I mentioned that I was also interested in entertainment media. Well, my involvement in *Dry* was what sparked my interest.

In early 2015, I got a call from a good friend and brother of mine, Linus Idahosa, Stephanie's husband. He told me how his wife had written and put an entire movie project together, and that they needed to shoot a good part of the movie overseas. Well, I had never been involved in a movie project and at that stage I didn't even know how to hold a movie camera, let alone understand the process of film-making. I knew I loved watching movies, and scriptwriting is one of my hobbies because I enjoy playing with words in written dialogue. I asked for the script of the movie to be sent through to me, and I can remember reading it and my heart beating fast with utter shock. I couldn't believe that the script I was reading was also a perfect representation of the current reality that child brides face in Africa. It was unbelievable and horrifying that the medical condition Vesicovaginal Fistula (VVF), which the movie addressed, affected in excess of 2 million women in Africa. This condition can be congenital, but it is also often caused by childbirth or violent cases of rape. Right away I was hooked. I had to be involved in this project, even if all I had to do was tell everyone I possibly could about it. And boy, I did.

I had experienced first-hand how much could be achieved by using a university as a stepping stone and pilot partner for exciting projects, and I knew what I had to do. (Besides, re-engaging with universities is one of the benefits of being an alumnus, so that is exactly what I did.) And who better than a university to have the best support system for a movie of that size, especially if that university had a film school? This would give us access to equipment, a production crew of actual film students, appropriate locations and venues (all within walking distance), a cabal of volunteer extras who just want to show their faces in the film – and an amazing venue to screen and host a movie premiere after all the work had been done. A university was the perfect partner for the overseas production of *Dry*, and that is how Aberystwyth University got involved in the project. Here I must give my absolute thanks to people like Ruth Owen Lewis, Murtza Ali Ghaznavi, Professor John Grattan, Susan Jenkins and the very many university staff and students who supported the process. It was a crowning glory when *Dry* picked up several international awards, including Best Overall Movie at the 2016 Africa Magic Viewers' Choice Awards. Imagine what happened afterwards? I started working on another movie project – and yes, you guessed right, I am also involving another university partner, because this time it is an education-focused movie.

But enough about my movie career. You have been bombarded with a lot of information by this stage and you are probably feeling overloaded with practical facts and experiences. I imagine you are now wondering what you should really do next. *The Graduate Code* was not written to confound and confuse you but to propound and enthuse you. If you are feeling confused, we need to sort that out. So I have developed the 4Ps of Action to help you at this stage. These are:

1 Probe
2 Prioritise
3 Plan
4 Push

Let's start with *probing*. This book has given you a lot of information and encouraged you to question your future career plans by working through a list of activities at the end of every chapter. If you have read the whole book and have completed the exercises, what you have essentially been doing is probing. (If you have not answered any of these questions, I am sorry to say that you need to go back to the beginning and start doing the activities. Just trust in the process.)

My point is that you need to probe first. The idea is that you start to figure things out by reading this book and responding to the activities. You start to appreciate some things you have never done, and to acknowledge some of your strengths (and maybe even failures). It is almost like getting you back to ground zero. And if you are already in tune with the activities, then they will get you to think about things a little differently. Even if you are totally covered and well aligned, and the book is not directly relevant to you, maybe you can still probe just to learn how to help another young person who is confused.

Now the second thing is to *prioritise*. This is very important. I appreciate that there are a lot of things to get through, especially when there are 22 chapters to read. To think you can totally fulfil all of these chapters would be pushing it, from my experience. Don't forget that these tenets have come together after a long process of engaging with young people and companies, gathering experiences and making mistakes over several years. You would be lying to yourself if you think you can make everything happen within a short space of time. Also, it is crucial to understand what stage you are in at the moment and which resources you have at your beck and call. And of course you are probably either a current student or working in an organisation that has its own demands on your time, so you need to figure out what it is you can do within the resources and time you have available to you. If you have a lot of both available now, then please feel free to get on with working through the whole book.

Another point to note is that some things will not be relevant to you right this minute and that you will need some time to put others in place or even backtrack. So how you use the code depends on where you are right at this moment. This is why prioritising is absolutely crucial. It is about arranging the 22 chapters in the order most useful to you, looking at which you can tackle immediately and which you need to come back to later.

Then my third action point is *plan*. Do not confuse prioritising and planning. They are totally different. To prioritise is to arrange the chapters of the Graduate Code in order of possible performance based on the time and resources you have available. But once that order is clear to you, you need to map out how you will deliver each chapter with timelines, proposed duration of delivery, the resources needed to deliver them and how and when you will get these resources. You also need to plan specific activities (and maybe even sub-activities within actions) so that you can identify if you are progressing or procrastinating. A good way to do this is to identify *career action milestones*, which are specific outcomes you ought to have achieved at a particular time.

Finally, there is *push*, and this one is pretty straightforward. Once you have a strong plan in place, all that remains is for you to push and proceed. As you push, you need to keep referring to your priorities and plan to make sure you are on schedule, on target and in line with these priorities.

I always thought I would complete this book with a big bang. So how about we end it with a poem?

> Now that you've read *The Graduate Code*
> Though the pressures are mounting like a load
> There are practical ideas contained within
> Instructions and activities to help you win
> May you be bright and may you be bold
> As I wish you success and career gold.

· ·

ACTIVITY 22

22a. Prioritise the entire Graduate Code. Considering the available time and resources you have right now, outline the five chapters you are most likely to act on.

22b. Draw up a plan of action based on your priorities listed in 22a. In your plan, list the following: main activities, sub-activities, proposed timeline/duration of delivery, milestones and the resources you will need to achieve your milestones.

NOTES

NOTES

NOTES

NOTES

NOTES